JUL '91 SX19.95

THE LANGUAGE
OF MORALS

BY

R. M. HARE

D0078073

CLARENDON PRESS · OXFORD

Oxford University Press, Walton Street, Oxford OX2 6DP

Oxford New York Toronto
Delhi Bombay Calcutta Madras Karachi
Petaling Jaya Singapore Hong Kong Tokyo
Nairobi Dar es Salaam Cape Town
Melbourne Auckland

and associated companies in
Berlin Ibadan

Oxford is a trade mark of Oxford University Press

ISBN 0–19–881077–6

First published by the Clarendon Press 1952
First issued as an Oxford University Press Paperback 1964
Seventh impression 1990

All rights reserved. No part of this publication may be reproduced,
stored in a retrieval system, or transmitted, in any form or by any means,
electronic, mechanical, photocopying, recording, or otherwise, without
the prior permission of Oxford University Press

This book is sold subject to the condition that it shall not, by way
of trade or otherwise, be lent, re-sold, hired out or otherwise circulated
without the publisher's prior consent in any form of binding or cover
other than that in which it is published and without a similar condition
including this condition being imposed on the subsequent purchaser

Printed and bound in
Great Britain by Biddles Ltd,
Guildford and King's Lynn

PREFACE

I HAVE set out in this book to write a clear, brief, and readable introduction to ethics which shall bring the beginner as directly as possible to grips with the fundamental problems of the subject. I have therefore, in reducing the material which I had prepared to about half its original length, left out most of those qualifications, answers to minor objections, and other defences with which the security-minded philosopher is apt to hedge himself round. Though I think that the approach to ethics which is sketched in these pages is in general a fruitful one, I shall be less disturbed if my readers disagree with me than if they fail to understand me. Almost every paragraph in this book, as in other works of philosophy, requires some qualification; but to supply it on every occasion would be to make my main contentions difficult to grasp. I have therefore tried to adopt throughout as definite a standpoint as possible, in the belief that it is more important that there should be discussion of the points herein raised, than that I should survive it unscathed.

Ethics, as I conceive it, is the logical study of the language of morals. It is in general easier to understand the very complex logic of moral terms if one has some acquaintance with the simpler kinds of logic; but since many students of philosophy are for some reason made to study ethics without such acquaintance, I have tried not to take it for granted. If anyone approaches this book without any previous philosophical reading, he will, I hope, find it intelligible if he follows this simple rule: to omit any passages which he finds difficult, go on reading, and return to them later. I have included, for the benefit of those who may be interested in them, certain very cursory references to some of the familiar 'types of ethical theory', and also to the works of some of the best-known writers on ethics; but these references may be ignored without missing any essential of my argument. I have put the section on 'The Imperative Mood' first, because it seems to me the most fundamental; but since it is also perhaps the most difficult, I have, in Part II, not taken for granted the argument of Part I; any reader, therefore, who wishes to take these two parts in the reverse order is at liberty to do so.

I have deliberately avoided references to the problems of moral psychology. In particular, the problem known as 'The Freedom of the Will', which has a place in most introductions to ethics, is not mentioned, and the problem usually referred to by Aristotle's title *Akrasia*, which should be discussed more often than it is, is mentioned only in passing. This is not because I consider these problems unimportant, nor because I have nothing to say about them, but because they are rather problems of the language of the psychology of morals, than of the language of morals itself.

My thanks are due, in the first place, to the Master and Scholars of Balliol College, for their generosity in giving me, during the year 1950–1, the relief from my teaching duties without which the task could never have been completed. Secondly, I have to thank the examiners of the T. H. Green Moral Philosophy Prize, Professors H. J. Paton and G. Ryle, and Mr. P. H. Nowell-Smith, for their many helpful comments on my dissertation for the prize, of which Part I of this book is an abridgement. Thirdly, I owe acknowledgement to those many at Oxford and elsewhere, in the course of discussion with whom I have learnt most of what is here set out; my debt to Mr. J. O. Urmson, for example, will be obvious. I have especial reason to be grateful to Mr. D. Mitchell and Professors H. L. A. Hart, A. J. Ayer and A. E. Duncan-Jones, who have read part or all of my typescript and saved me from serious errors—for those which may remain I ask forgiveness. The latter's paper to the Aristotelian Society on 'Assertions and Commands' appeared too late to allow any comment in the text; and the same is true of Professor

Everett Hall's book *What is Value?*, in which the subject of
the present book is examined on a more ambitious scale.
For a discussion of Professor Hall's views I must refer the
reader to a forthcoming review in *Mind*. I have also to
thank Mr. B. F. McGuinness for help in compiling the Index.
Lastly, in case brevity should seem to have led to dogmatism
in dealing with the writings of philosophers both living and
dead, and to injustice towards their doctrines, I must confess
that I have learnt as much from those writers with whom I
may appear to disagree, as from those whom I applaud.

I dedicate this study of moral language to those good men
and women without whose lives the moralist would be wast-
ing his breath, and especially to my wife.

R. M. H.

BALLIOL COLLEGE
   1952

In the second impression I have made some minor correc-
tions which did not involve radical disturbance of the text.
Were I rewriting the book, I should write it differently, since
now I have the advantage of knowing what has been misunderstood, and what has misled. Though my views have
changed in some particulars, they have not changed in any
respect which seems to me fundamental. I am most grateful to those who have helped to clarify these issues by com-
menting on my arguments. For my present views, I must
refer the reader to a new book, a continuation of this, which
I hope to publish shortly. *

R. M. H.

BALLIOL COLLEGE
   1960

* *Freedom and Reason* (Clarendon Press, 1963).

CONTENTS

PART I

THE IMPERATIVE MOOD

'Virtue, then, is a disposition governing our choices'.

ARISTOTLE, *Eth. Nic.* 1106^b 36

1

PRESCRIPTIVE LANGUAGE

1. 1. IF we were to ask of a person 'What are his moral principles?' the way in which we could be most sure of a true answer would be by studying what he *did*. He might, to be sure, profess in his conversation all sorts of principles, which in his actions he completely disregarded; but it would be when, knowing all the relevant facts of a situation, he was faced with choices or decisions between alternative courses of action, between alternative answers to the question 'What shall I do?', that he would reveal in what principles of conduct he really believed. The reason why actions are in a peculiar way revelatory of moral principles is that the function of moral principles is to guide conduct. The language of morals is one sort of prescriptive language. And this is what makes ethics worth studying: for the question 'What shall I do?' is one that we cannot for long evade; the problems of conduct, though sometimes less diverting than crossword puzzles, *have to be solved* in a way that crossword puzzles do not. We cannot wait to see the solution in the next issue, because on the solution of the problems depends what happens in the next issue. Thus, in a world in which the problems of conduct become every day more complex and tormenting, there is a great need for an understanding of the language in which these problems are posed and answered. For confusion about our moral language leads, not merely to theoretical muddles, but to needless practical perplexities.

An old-fashioned, but still useful, way of studying anything is *per genus et differentiam*; if moral language belongs to the genus 'prescriptive language', we shall most easily understand its nature if we compare and contrast first of all prescriptive language with other sorts of language, and then moral language with other sorts of prescriptive language. That, in brief, is the plan of this book. I shall proceed from the simple to the more complex. I shall deal first with the simplest form of prescriptive language, the ordinary imperative sentence. The logical behaviour of this type of sentence is of great interest to the student of moral language because, in spite of its comparative simplicity, it raises in an easily discernible form many of the problems which have beset ethical theory. Therefore, although it is no part of my purpose to 'reduce' moral language to imperatives, the study of imperatives is by far the best introduction to the study of ethics; and if the reader does not at once see the relevance to ethics of the earlier part of the discussion, I must ask him to be patient. Neglect of the principles enunciated in the first part of this book is the source of many of the most insidious confusions in ethics.

From singular imperatives I shall proceed to universal imperatives or principles. The discussion of these, and of how we come to adopt or reject them, will give me an opportunity of describing the processes of teaching and learning, and the logic of the language that we use for these purposes. Since one of the most important uses of moral language is in moral teaching, the relevance of this discussion to ethics will be obvious.

I shall then go on to discuss a kind of prescriptive language which is more nearly related to the language of morals than is the simple imperative. This is the language of non-moral value-judgements—all those sentences containing words like 'ought', 'right', and 'good' which are not moral judgements. I shall seek to establish that many of the features which have caused trouble to students of ethics are also displayed by these sorts of sentence—so much so that a proper understanding of them does much to elucidate the problems of ethics itself. I shall take the two most typical moral words 'good' and 'ought' in turn, and shall discuss first their non-moral uses, and then their moral ones; in each case I hope to show that these uses have many features in common. In conclusion I shall relate the logic of 'ought' and 'good', in both moral and non-moral contexts, to the logic of imperatives by constructing a logical model in which artificial concepts, which could to some extent do duty for the value-words of ordinary language, are defined in terms of a modified imperative mood. This model is not to be taken too seriously; it is intended only as a very rough schematization of the preceding discussion, which itself contains the substance of what I have to say.

Thus the classification of prescriptive language which I propose may be represented as follows:

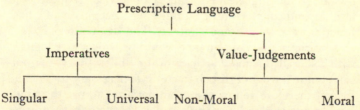

This classification is rough only; it will be made more precise in the course of the book; for example, it will be seen that the so-called 'universal imperatives' of ordinary language are not proper universals. Nor do I wish to suggest that the classification is exhaustive; there are, for example, many different kinds of singular imperatives, and of non-moral value-judgements; and there are other kinds of imperatives besides singular and universal. But the classification is good enough to begin with, and explains the plan of this book.

1. 2. The writers of elementary grammar books sometimes classify sentences according as they express statements, commands, or questions. This classification is not exhaustive or rigorous enough for the logician. For example, logicians have devoted much labour to showing that sentences in the indicative mood may be of very various logical characters, and that the classification of them all under the one name 'statements' may lead to serious error if it makes us ignore the important differences between them. We shall in the later part of this book see how one kind of indicative sentence, that which expresses value-judgements, behaves logically in a quite different way from the ordinary indicative sentence.

Imperatives, likewise, are a mixed bunch. Even if we exclude sentences like 'Would I were in Grantchester!' which are dealt with by some grammarians in the same division of their books as imperatives, we still have, among sentences that are in the imperative mood proper, many different kinds of utterance. We have military orders (parade-ground and otherwise), architects' specifications, instructions for cooking omelets or operating vacuum cleaners, pieces of advice, requests, entreaties, and countless other sorts of sentence, many of whose functions shade into one another. The distinction between these various kinds of sentence would provide a nice logician with material for many articles in the philosophical periodicals; but in a work of this character it is necessary to be bold. I shall therefore follow the grammarians and use the single term 'command' to cover all these sorts of thing that sentences in the imperative mood express, and within the class of commands make only some very broad distinctions. The justification for this procedure is that I hope to interest the reader in features that are common to all, or nearly all, these types of sentence; with their differences he is no doubt familiar enough. For the same reason I shall use the word 'statement' to cover whatever is expressed by typical indicative sentences, if there be such. I shall be drawing a contrast, that is to say, between sentences like 'Shut the door' and sentences like 'You are going to shut the door'.

It is difficult to deny that there is a difference between statements and commands; but it is far harder to say just what the difference is. It is not merely one of grammatical form; for if we had to study a newly discovered language we should be able to identify those grammatical forms which were used for expressing statements and commands respectively, and should call these forms 'indicative' and 'imperative' (if the language were constructed in such a way as to make this distinction useful). The distinction lies between the meanings which the different grammatical forms convey. Both are used for talking about a subject-matter, but they are used for talking about it in different ways. The two sentences 'You are going to shut the door' and 'Shut the door' are both about your shutting the door in the immediate future; but what they say about it is quite different. An indicative sentence is used for telling someone that something is the case; an imperative is not—it is used for telling someone to make something the case.

1. 3. It is well worth the moral philosopher's while examining some of the theories which have been, or which might be, held about the way in which imperatives have meaning. They offer a most arresting parallel to similar theories about moral judgements, and this parallel indicates that there may be some important logical similarity between the two. Let us first consider two theories, similar to the type of ethical theory to which I shall later give the name 'naturalist' (5. 3). Both are attempts to 'reduce' imperatives to indicatives. The first does this by representing them as expressing statements about the mind of the speaker. Just as it has been held that 'A is right' means 'I approve of A', so it might be held that 'Shut the door' means 'I want you to shut the door'. There is on the colloquial plane no harm in saying this; but it may be very misleading philosophically. It has the consequence that if I say 'Shut the door' and you say (to

the same person) 'Do not shut the door', we are not contradicting one another; and this is odd. The upholder of the
theory may reply that although there is no contradiction,
there is a disagreement in wishes, and that this is sufficient to
account for the feeling we have that the two sentences are
somehow incompatible with one another (that 'not' has the
same function as in the sentence 'You are not going to shut
the door'). But there remains the difficulty that the sentence
'Shut the door' seems to be about shutting the door, and not
about the speaker's frame of mind, just as instructions for
cooking omelets ('Take four eggs, &c.') are instructions about
eggs, not introspective analyses of the psyche of Mrs. Beeton.
To say that 'Shut the door' means the same as 'I want you to
shut the door' is like saying that 'You are going to shut the
door' means the same as 'I believe that you are going to shut
the door'. In both cases it seems strange to represent a remark about shutting the door as a remark about what is going
on in my mind. But in fact neither the word 'believe' nor
the word 'want' will bear this interpretation. 'I believe that
you are going to shut the door' is not (except in a highly
figurative way) a statement about my mind; it is a tentative
statement about your shutting the door, a more hesitant version of 'You are going to shut the door'; and similarly, 'I want
you to shut the door' is not a statement about my mind but
a polite way of saying the imperative 'Shut the door'. Unless
we understand the logic of 'You are going to shut the door',
we cannot understand the logic of 'I believe that you are going
to shut the door'; and similarly unless we understand 'Shut
the door' we are unlikely to understand 'I want you to shut
the door'. The theory, therefore, explains nothing; and the
parallel ethical theory is in the same case; for 'I approve of
A' is merely a more complicated and circumlocutory way of
saying 'A is right'. It is not a statement, verifiable by observation, that I have a recognizable feeling or recurrent frame of
mind; it is a value-judgement; if I ask 'Do I approve of A?'

my answer is a moral decision, not an observation of intro-
spectible fact. 'I approve of A' would be unintelligible to
someone who did not understand 'A is right', and the
explanation is a case of *obscurum per obscurius*.

1. 4. The second attempt to reduce imperatives to indicatives which I wish to consider is that of Dr. H. G. Bohnert.[1]
This interesting suggestion may be summarized (I hope
without injustice) by the statement that 'Shut the door' means
the same as 'Either you are going to shut the door, or X will
happen', where X is understood to be something bad for the
person addressed. A similar theory would be that it meant
the same as 'If you do not shut the door, X will happen'. This
theory is parallel to ethical theories of the sort which equate
'A is right' with 'A is conducive to Y' where Y is something
regarded by the generality as good, for example pleasure or the
avoidance of pain. We shall see later that value-expressions
sometimes acquire—by reason of the constancy of the standards by which they are applied—a certain descriptive force;
thus if, in a society whose standards are markedly utilita-
rian, we say 'The Health Service has done a lot of good',
everyone knows that we are implying that the Health Service
has averted a lot of pain, anxiety, &c. Similarly, in the case of
imperatives which are to a high degree 'hypothetical' (3. 2)
because we quickly realize, to the attainment of what end,
or the prevention of what untoward result, they are directed,
Bohnert's analysis is plausible. To take his own example,
'Run', said in a burning house, is somewhat similar in intention to 'Either you run or you burn'. But in cases where
the end aimed at is not so easily recognized (the imperative
being only to a small degree, or not at all, 'hypothetical') the
hearer may be quite at a loss to understand, on this analysis,
what he is to supply after the word 'or'. It is very difficult to
see how a sentence like 'Please tell your father that I called'

[1] 'The Semiotic Status of Commands', *Philosophy of Science*, xii (1945),
302.

would be analysed on Bohnert's theory. It is, of course, always possible to terminate the analysis 'or something bad will happen'; but this expedient succeeds only by reintroducing into the analysis a prescriptive word; for 'bad' is a value-word, and therefore prescriptive. And similarly, teleological theories of ethics which interpret 'right' as 'conducive to Z', where 'Z' is a value-word such as 'satisfaction' or 'happiness', only store up for themselves the difficulty of analysing such words.

The temptation to reduce imperatives to indicatives is very strong, and has the same source as the temptation to analyse value-words in the way called 'naturalistic'. This is the feeling that the 'proper' indicative sentence, of which there is thought to be only one kind, is somehow above suspicion in a way that other sorts of sentence are not; and that therefore, in order to put these other sorts of sentence above suspicion, it is necessary to show that they are *really* indicatives. This feeling was intensified when the so-called 'verificationist' theory of meaning became popular. This theory, which is in many ways a very fruitful one in its proper sphere, holds, to put it roughly, that a sentence does not have meaning unless there is something that would be the case if it were true. Now this is a very promising account of one of the ways in which a certain class of sentences (the typical indicatives) have meaning. Obviously, if a sentence is claimed to express a statement of fact, and yet we have no idea what would be the case if it were true, then that sentence is (to us) meaningless. But if this criterion of meaningfulness, which is useful in the case of statements of fact, is applied indiscriminately to types of utterance which are not intended to express statements of fact, trouble will result. Imperative sentences do not satisfy this criterion, and it may be that sentences expressing moral judgements do not either; but this only shows that they do not express statements in the sense defined by the criterion; and this sense may be a narrower one than that of normal usage. It does not mean that they are meaningless, or even that their meaning is of such a character that no logical rules can be given for their employment.[1]

1. 5. The feeling, that only 'proper indicatives' are above suspicion, can survive (surprisingly) the discovery that there are perfectly good significant sentences of our ordinary speech which are not reducible to indicatives. It survives in the assumption that any meaning which is discovered for these sentences must necessarily be of some logically inferior status to that of indicatives. This assumption has led philosophers such as Professor A. J. Ayer, in the course of expounding their most valuable researches into the logical nature of moral judgements, to make incidental remarks which have raised needless storms of protest.[2] The substance of Ayer's theory is that moral judgements do not ordinarily function in the same way as the class of indicative sentences marked out by his verification-criterion. But by his way of stating his view, and his assimilation of moral judgements to other (quite distinct) types of sentence which are also marked off from typical indicatives by this criterion, he stirred up dust which has not yet subsided. All this might be closely paralleled by a similar treatment of imperatives—and it seems that writers of the same general line of thought as Ayer would have said the same sort of thing about imperatives as they did about moral judgements. Suppose that we recognize the obvious fact that imperatives are not like typical indicatives. Suppose, further, that we regard only typical indicatives as above suspicion. It will be natural then to say 'Imperatives do not state anything, they only express wishes'. Now to say that imperatives express wishes is, like the first theory which we considered, unexceptionable on the colloquial plane; we would indeed say,

[1] See my article 'Imperative Sentences', *Mind*, lviii (1949), 21, from which some material is here used.

[2] See especially *Language, Truth and Logic*, 2nd ed., pp. 108–9. For a later and more balanced statement, see 'On the Analysis of Moral Judgments', *Philosophical Essays*, pp. 231 ff.

if someone said 'Keep my name out of this', that he had expressed a wish to have his name kept out of it. But nevertheless the extreme ambiguity of the word 'express' may generate
philosophical confusion. We speak of expressing statements,
opinions, beliefs, mathematical relations, and so on; and if it
is in one of these senses that the word is used, the theory,
though it tells us little, is harmless. But unfortunately it is
also used in ways which are unlike these; and Ayer's use (in
speaking of moral judgements) of the word 'evince' as its
rough synonym was dangerous. Artists and composers and
poets are said to express their own and our feelings; oaths
are said to express anger; and dancing upon the table may
express joy. Thus to say that imperatives express wishes may
lead the unwary to suppose that what happens when we use
one, is this: we have welling up inside us a kind of longing,
to which, when the pressure gets too great for us to bear, we
give vent by saying an imperative sentence. Such an interpretation, when applied to such sentences as 'Supply and fit
to door mortise dead latch and plastic knob furniture', is unplausible. And it would seem that value-judgements also may
fail to satisfy the verification-criterion, and indeed be in some
sense, like imperatives, prescriptive, without having this sort
of thing said about them. It is perfectly unexceptionable, on
the colloquial plane, to say that the sentence 'A is good' is
used to express approval of A (*The Shorter Oxford English
Dictionary* says: 'Approve: . . . to pronounce to be good');
but it is philosophically misleading if we think that the
approval which is expressed is a peculiar warm feeling inside
us. If the Minister of Local Government expresses approval
of my town plan by getting his underlings to write to me
saying 'The Minister approves of your plan' or 'The Minister
thinks your plan is the best one', I shall in no circumstances
confirm the letter by getting a private detective to observe
the Minister for signs of emotion. In this case, to have such
a letter sent *is* to approve.

1. 6. There could be no analogue, in the case of singular imperatives, of the 'attitude' variety of the approval theory of value-judgements;[1] but it is possible to construct such a theory about *universal* imperative sentences. If someone said 'Never hit a man when he is down', it would be natural to say that he had expressed a certain attitude towards such conduct. It is extremely hard to define exactly this attitude or give criteria for recognizing it, just as it is difficult to say exactly what *moral* approval is as opposed to other sorts of approval. The only safe way of characterizing the attitude which is expressed by a universal imperative is to say 'The attitude that one should not (or should) do so and so'; and the only safe way of characterizing the attitude which is expressed by a moral judgement is to say 'The attitude that it is wrong (or right) to do so and so'. To maintain an attitude of 'moral approval' towards a certain practice is to have a disposition to think, on the appropriate occasions, that it is right; or, if 'think' itself is a dispositional word, it is simply to think that it is right; and our thinking that it is right may be betrayed or exhibited—behaviourists would say constituted—by our acting in certain ways (above all, doing acts of the sort in question when the occasion arises; next, saying that they are right; applauding them in other ways, and so on). But there is in all this nothing to explain just *what* one thinks when one thinks that a certain sort of act is right. And similarly, if we said that 'Never hit a man when he is down' expressed an attitude that one should not hit, &c. (or an attitude of aversion from hitting, or a 'contra-attitude' towards hitting), we should not have said anything that would be intelligible to someone who did not understand the sentence which we were trying to explain.

I wish to emphasize that I am not seeking to refute any of these theories. They have all of them the characteristic that, if put in everyday terms, they say nothing exceptionable so

[1] See, for example, C. L. Stevenson, *Ethics and Language*.

far as their main contentions go; but when we seek to understand how they explain the philosophical perplexities which
generated them, we are either forced to interpret them in
such a way as to render them unplausible, or else find that
they merely set the same problems in a more complicated way.
Sentences containing the word 'approve' are so difficult of
analysis that it seems perverse to use this notion to explain
the meaning of moral judgements which we learn to make
years before we learn the word 'approve'; and similarly, it
would be perverse to explain the meaning of the imperative
mood in terms of wishing or any other feeling or attitude;
for we learn how to respond to and use commands long before
we learn the comparatively complex notions of 'wish', 'desire',
'aversion', &c.

1. 7. We must now consider another group of theories
which have often been held concurrently with the group just
considered. These hold that the function in language of
either moral judgements or imperatives (which the theories
often equate) is to affect causally the behaviour or emotions
of the hearer. Professor R. Carnap writes:

> But actually a value-statement is nothing else than a command
> in a misleading grammatical form. It may have effects upon the
> actions of men, and these effects may either be in accordance with
> our wishes or not; but it is neither true nor false.[1]

and Professor Ayer writes:

> Ethical terms do not serve only to express feeling. They are
> calculated also to arouse feeling, and so to stimulate action. Indeed
> some of them are used in such a way as to give the sentences in
> which they occur the effect of commands.[2]

More recently this sort of view has been elaborated by Professor Stevenson.[3] Here again we have a type of theory which
may be on the colloquial plane harmless, but which suggests

---

[1] *Philosophy and Logical Syntax*, p. 24.
[2] *Language, Truth and Logic*, 2nd ed., p. 108.
[3] *Ethics and Language*, especially p. 21.

philosophical errors by seeming to assimilate the processes of using a command or a moral judgement to other processes which are in fact markedly dissimilar.

It is indeed true of imperative sentences that if anyone, in using them, is being sincere or honest, he intends that the person referred to should *do* something (namely, what is commanded). This is indeed a test of sincerity in the case of commands, just as a statement is held to be sincere only if the speaker believes it. And there are similar criteria, as we shall later see, for sincerely assenting to commands and statements that have been given or made by someone else. But this is not quite what the theories suggest. They suggest, rather, that the function of a command is to affect the hearer causally, or get him to do something; and to say this may be misleading. In ordinary parlance there is no harm in saying that in using a command our intention is to get someone to do something; but for philosophical purposes an important distinction has to be made. The processes of *telling* someone to do something, and *getting* him to do it, are quite distinct, logically, from each other.[1] The distinction may be elucidated by considering a parallel one in the case of statements. To tell someone that something is the case is logically distinct from getting (or trying to get) him to believe it. Having told someone that something is the case we may, if he is not disposed to believe what we say, start on a quite different process of trying to get him to believe it (trying to persuade or convince him that what we have said is true). No one, in seeking to explain the function of indicative sentences, would say that they were attempts to persuade someone that something is the case. And there is no more reason for saying that commands are attempts to persuade or get someone to do something; here, too, we first tell someone what he is to do, and

---

[1] For a fuller treatment of this question see my article, 'Freedom of the Will', *Aristotelian Society*, Supplementary Vol. xxv (1951), 201, from which I have used some material here and in 10. 3.

then, if he is not disposed to do what we say, we may start on the wholly different process of trying to get him to do it. Thus the instruction already quoted 'Supply and fit to door mortise dead latch and plastic knob furniture' is not intended to *galvanize* joiners into activity; for such a purpose other means are employed.

This distinction is important for moral philosophy; for in fact the suggestion, that the function of moral judgements was to persuade, led to a difficulty in distinguishing their function from that of propaganda.[1] Since I am going to draw attention to some similarities between commands and moral judgements, and to classify them both as prescriptions, I require most emphatically to dissociate myself from the confusion of either of these things with propaganda. We have here, as often in philosophy, a mixture of two distinctions. The first is that between the language of statements and prescriptive language. The second is that between telling someone something and getting him to believe or do what one has told him. That these two distinctions are quite different, and overlap each other, should be clear after a moment's consideration. For we may tell someone, either that something is the case, or to do something; here there is no attempt at persuasion (or influencing or inducing or getting to). If the person is not disposed to assent to what we tell him, we may then resort to rhetoric, propaganda, marshalling of additional facts, psychological tricks, threats, bribes, torture, mockery, promises of protection, and a variety of other expedients. All of these are ways of inducing him or getting him to do something; the first four are also ways of getting him to believe something; none of them are ways of telling him something, though those of them which involve the employment of language may include telling him all sorts of things. Regarded as inducements or expedients for persuasion, their success is judged solely by their effects—by whether the person believes

[1] Cf. Stevenson, *Ethics and Language*, ch. xi.

or does what we are trying to get him to believe or do. It does not matter whether the means used to persuade him are fair or foul, so long as they do persuade him. And therefore the natural reaction to the realization that someone is trying to persuade us is 'He's trying to get at me; I must be on my guard; I mustn't let him bias my decision unfairly; I must be careful to make up my own mind in the matter and remain a free responsible agent'. Such a reaction to moral judgements should not be encouraged by philosophers. On the other hand, these are not natural reactions either to someone's telling us that something is the case, or to his telling us to do something (for example, to fit a latch to the door). Telling someone to do something, or that something is the case, is answering the question 'What shall I do?' or 'What are the facts?' When we have answered these questions the hearer knows what to do or what the facts are—if what we have told him is right. He is not necessarily thereby *influenced* one way or the other, nor have we failed if he is not; for he may decide to disbelieve or disobey us, and the mere telling him does nothing—and seeks to do nothing—to prevent him doing this. But persuasion is not directed to a person as a rational agent, who is asking himself (or us) 'What shall I do?'; it is not an answer to this or to any other question; it is an attempt to *make* him answer it in a particular way.

It is easy to see, therefore, why the so-called 'imperative theory' of moral judgements raised the protests that it did. Because based on a misconception of the function, not only of moral judgements but also of the commands to which they were being assimilated, it seemed to impugn the rationality of moral discourse. But if we realize that commands, however much they may differ from statements, are like them in this, that they consist in telling someone something, not in seeking to influence him, it does no harm to draw attention to the similarities between commands and moral judgements. For, as I shall show, commands, because they, like statements, are essentially intended for answering questions asked by rational agents, are governed by logical rules just as statements are. And this means that moral judgements may also be so governed. We remember that the greatest of all rationalists, Kant, referred to moral judgements as imperatives; though we must remember also that he was using the latter term in an extended sense, and that moral judgements, though they are like imperatives in some respects, are unlike them in others (11. 5).

2

IMPERATIVES AND LOGIC

2. 1. In order to characterize clearly the difference between imperatives and indicatives, it will be helpful so to analyse the two types of sentence, as to make it plain what elements of meaning they have in common, and so isolate the essential difference. Since I have already attempted to do this in an article referred to above (1. 4), I shall be as brief as possible.

We have noticed that the two sentences 'You are going to shut the door' and 'Shut the door' are both about the same thing, namely, your shutting the door in the immediate future; but that they are used to say different things about it. It is purely an accident of grammar that those parts of the spoken or written sentence which, in either case, refer to this thing that they are about, are not identical. Let us recast the sentences more clearly by writing in both cases an identical phrase for referring to this thing that they are both about. The phrase might be:

Your shutting the door in the immediate future.

We shall then have to add something, different in each case, which supplies the rest of what each sentence conveys. What we have so far tells us quite clearly what the sentences are about. It does not, however, tell us what the speaker is saying about it. We do not know whether he is stating that your shutting the door in the immediate future is what is going to happen or be the case, or whether he is telling us to make it the case, or something else. In order to complete the sentences, therefore, something has to be added to tell us this. We might complete the sentences as a command or a statement respectively, by writing:

Your shutting the door in the immediate future, please.
Your shutting the door in the immediate future, yes.

These two sentences would correspond to the normal English
sentences:

Shut the door.
You are going to shut the door.

We shall need technical terms for referring to these different parts of sentences. The terms adopted in my article are
not altogether satisfactory, and therefore I shall coin entirely
new words. I shall call the part of the sentence that is common to both moods ('Your shutting the door in the immediate
future') the *phrastic*; and the part that is different in the case
of commands and statements ('yes' or 'please'), the *neustic*.
Readers of Liddell and Scott's *Greek Lexicon* will recognize
the appropriateness of these terms. 'Phrastic' is derived from
a Greek word meaning 'to point out or indicate', and 'neustic'
from a word meaning 'to nod assent'. Both words are used
indifferently of imperative and indicative speech. The utterance of a sentence containing phrastic and neustic might be
dramatized as follows: (1) The speaker points out or indicates
what he is going to state to be the case, or command to be
made the case; (2) He nods, as if to say 'It *is* the case', or 'Do
it'. He will, however, have to nod in a different way, according as he means one or other of these things.

2. 2. Now clearly, if we are looking for the essential difference between statements and commands, we have to look in
the neustic, not in the phrastic. But, as the use of the single
word 'neustic' indicates, there is still something in common
between indicative and imperative neustics. This is the common notion of, so to speak, 'nodding' a sentence. It is something that is done by anyone who uses a sentence in earnest,
and does not merely mention it or quote it in inverted commas; something essential to *saying* (and meaning) anything.
The absence of inverted commas in written language sym-
bolizes the element of meaning of which I am speaking; to
write a sentence without inverted commas is like signing a

cheque; to write it within inverted commas is like drawing
a cheque without signing it, e.g. to show someone how to
draw cheques. We could have a convention that, instead of
putting inverted commas round sentences that we were men-
tioning and not using, we nodded, or made some special
mark in writing, when we *were* using a sentence in earnest. The
'assertion symbol' in the logical system of Frege and in that
of Russell and Whitehead has, among other functions, this
one of signifying the use or affirmation of a sentence.[1] It
could, in this function, be applied to commands as well as to
statements. We may perhaps strain language slightly and use
the word 'affirm' of both.

Closely allied to such an affirmation sign would be a sign
for agreement or assent for use by a hearer. To use such a sign
of assent would be tantamount to repeating the sentence with
the pronouns, &c., changed where necessary. Thus, if I said
'You are going to shut the door', and you answered 'Yes',
this would be a sign of assent, and would be equivalent to
'I am going to shut the door'. And if I said 'Shut the door',
and you answered 'Aye, aye sir', this likewise would be a
sign of assent; if we wished to express what it is equivalent
to, we might say 'Let me shut the door' or 'I will shut the
door' (where 'I will' is not a prediction but the expression of
a resolve or a promise). Now this should give us a clue to the
essential difference between statements and commands; it
lies in what is involved in assenting to them; and what is involved in assenting to them is, as I have said, closely allied
to what is involved in affirming them in the first place.[2]

If we assent to a statement we are said to be sincere in our
assent if and only if we believe that it is true (believe what
the speaker has said). If, on the other hand, we assent to a

---

[1] See Russell and Whitehead, *Principia Mathematica*, i. 9.
[2] For some interesting remarks about the kindred notions of 'admitting'
and 'confirming', see P. F. Strawson, 'Truth', *Analysis* ix (1948–9), 83,
and *Aristotelian Society*, Supplementary vol. xxiv (1950), 129.

second-person command addressed to ourselves, we are said to be sincere in our assent if and only if we do or resolve to do what the speaker has told us to do; if we do not do it but only resolve to do it later, then if, when the occasion arises for doing it, we do not do it, we are said to have changed our mind; we are no longer sticking to the assent which we previously expressed. It is a tautology to say that we cannot sincerely assent to a second-person command addressed to ourselves, and *at the same time* not perform it, if now is the occasion for performing it and it is in our (physical and psychological) power to do so. Similarly, it is a tautology to say that we cannot sincerely assent to a statement, and *at the same time* not believe it. Thus we may characterize provisionally the difference between statements and commands by saying that, whereas sincerely assenting to the former involves *believing* something, sincerely assenting to the latter involves (on the appropriate occasion and if it is within our power), *doing* something. But this statement is over-simplified, and will require qualification later (11. 2).

In the case of third-person commands, to assent is to join in affirming. In the case of first-person commands ('Let me do so and so') and resolves ('I will do so and so'), which are closely similar to one another, affirmation and assent are identical. It is logically impossible for a man to dissent from what he himself is affirming (though of course he may not be sincere in affirming it).

2. 3. It must be explained that, as I am using the word 'affirm', it is not the opposite of 'negate'. It is possible to affirm either an affirmative sentence or a negative one. The sign of negation, 'not', is normally part of the phrastic of both indicatives and imperatives; thus, instead of 'You are not going to shut the door' we should write 'Your not shutting the door in the immediate future, yes'; and instead of 'Do not shut the door', we should write 'Your not shutting the door in the immediate future, please'. Modal sentences con-

taining the word 'may' could, it seems, be represented by
negating the neustic; thus 'You may shut the door' (per-
missive) might be written 'I don't tell you not to shut the
door' and this in turn might be rendered 'Your not shutting
the door in the immediate future, not-please'; and similarly,
the sentence 'You may be going to shut the door' might be
rendered 'I don't say you aren't going to shut the door' or
'Your not shutting the door in the immediate future, not-yes'.
But these are complications into which we need not enter.

I have indicated in the article already referred to that in
their ordinary uses the common logical connectives 'if', 'and',
and 'or', like the sign of negation, are best treated as part of
the phrastics of sentences. This means that they are common
ground between indicatives and imperatives. The same is
true, with a certain qualification to be mentioned later (11. 5),
of the quantifiers 'all' and 'some'. I am not now so sure that
in ordinary language these words behave, logically, in exactly
the same way in imperatives as they do in indicatives; but
be this as it may, the differences are purely an accident of
grammar. By using the ordinary logical connectives, as they
are used in the indicative mood, in the phrastics of our re-
modelled imperative sentences, we could do with the revised
imperative mood everything that we now do with the natural
one. This is clear from the fact that, by a circumlocution, we
could always, instead of a simple command (e.g. 'Shut the
door or put the door-stop in position', said to Jones) substitute the command to make an indicative sentence true
(e.g. 'Make the sentence "Jones is going to shut the door or
put the door-stop in position" true'). This, however, is not
to be construed as an admission of the logical 'primacy' of
the indicative mood (whatever that might mean); for we
could do the same the other way round—e.g. by saying, instead of 'Jones shut the door at 5 p.m.', 'The command
[actual or imagined] "Let Jones shut the door at 5 p.m." was
obeyed'. The only restriction on this procedure is due to the

fact, referred to later (12. 4), that the imperative mood is much less rich than the indicative, especially in tenses.

The imperative and the indicative moods also have in common, because of their common phrastic element, everything to do with their reference to actual or possible states of affairs. There is a possible state of affairs referred to by the phrastic 'Your shutting the door in the immediate future'. This reference is not affected by what comes after. Both imperatives and indicatives have to refer to the state of affairs which they are about. This means that imperatives, like indicatives, can suffer from the malady to which the so-called verification theory of meaning draws attention; for this malady, being a malady of the phrastic, has nothing to do with statements as such; those who thought so were misled. One of the ways in which a sentence can fail to signify is for it to refer to no identifiable state of affairs. Thus the sentences 'The Absolute is green' and 'Let the Absolute be made green' are meaningless for the same reason, namely, that we do not know what is referred to by 'The Absolute being green'. Sentences may also for this reason fail to be understood by one person, though perfectly significant to another; thus the command 'Luff' is meaningless to those who do not know what luffing consists in. It would be unfortunate if the verification criterion were thought to impugn the meaningfulness of all but indicative sentences—as if 'Shut the door' was as meaningless as 'Frump the bump'.

There is another malady to which imperatives, like indicatives, are liable, owing to the presence of logical connectives in the phrastics of both of them. This is called, in the case of indicatives, self-contradiction; and the term is equally applicable to imperatives. Commands as well as statements can contradict one another. Even if this were not a normal way of speaking, we might well adopt it; for the feature to which it draws attention in commands is identical with that which is normally called contradiction. Consider

the following example, taken from Lord Cunningham's auto-
biography.[1] The admiral and the captain of a cruiser which
is his flagship shout almost simultaneously to the helmsman
in order to avoid a collision, one 'Hard 'a port' and the other
'Hard 'a starboard'. Lord Cunningham refers to these two
orders as 'contrary'; and so they are, in the proper Aristotelian sense.[2] It follows that the two orders contradict one
another in the sense that the conjunction of them is self-
contradictory; the relation between them is the same as that
between the two predictions 'You are going to turn hard 'a
port' and 'You are going to turn hard 'a starboard'. Some
orders can, of course, be contradictory without being contrary; the simple contradictory of 'Shut the door' is 'Do not
shut the door'.

It might be held that the law of the excluded middle does
not apply to commands. This, however, is a mistake if it is
implied that commands are peculiar in this respect. It is quite
clear that if I do not say 'Shut the door' this does not compel
me, logically, to say 'Do not shut the door'. I can say 'You
may either shut the door or not shut the door'; or I can say
nothing at all. But similarly, if I do not say 'You are going to
shut the door', this does not compel me logically to say 'You
are not going to shut the door'. I can say 'You may be going
to shut the door, and you may be going not to shut the door',
or I can say nothing at all. But if asked 'Am I going to shut
the door or not?' I have to answer, because of the terms of the
question, either 'You are going to shut the door' or 'You are
not going to shut the door' unless I refuse to answer the question at all. 'You may be going to' is not an answer to this
question. And similarly, if I am asked 'Shall I shut the door
or not?' I have to answer, if I answer the question at all, either
'Shut it' or 'Don't shut it'. The truth is that our language
possesses ways of speaking in a three-valued way and ways

---

[1] Viscount Cunningham, *A Sailor's Odyssey*, p. 162.
[2] *Categories*, 6ᵃ 17.

of speaking in a two-valued way; and these two ways are available in both the indicative and the imperative moods.

Another way of showing that simple imperatives are normally two-valued is to point out that the advice (to a chess player) 'At your next move, either move your queen or don't move your queen' is analytic (I define this term below (3. 3)). It gives the player no positive instructions whatever as to what he is to do, just as the sentence 'It is either raining or not raining' tells me nothing about the weather.[1] If the logic of simple imperatives were three-valued, the sentence quoted would not be analytic; it would positively exclude a third possibility, that of neither moving the queen nor not moving her. Imperative disjunctions of this form are not always analytic; for example 'Either stay in or don't stay in' would naturally be taken to imply 'Don't stand blocking the doorway'; but this has nothing to do with the imperative as such; it is a feature of the phrastic of the sentence, as is shown by comparing the parallel indicative sentence 'You're going either to stay in or not stay in (*sc.* you're not going to stand dithering there in the doorway)'.

2. 4. It follows, from the fact that commands may contradict one another, that in order to avoid self-contradiction, a command, like a statement, must observe certain logical rules. These rules are the rules for the use of all the expressions contained in it. In the case of some expressions—the so-called logical words—these rules are what give the expressions all the meaning they have. Thus to know the meaning of the word 'all' is to know that one cannot without self-contradiction say certain things, for example 'All men are mortal and Socrates is a man but Socrates is not mortal'. If the reader will reflect, how he would tell whether someone knew the meaning of the word 'all', he will see that the only way he could do it would be by finding out what simpler sentences that person thought were entailed by sentences containing the word 'all'. 'Entailed'

[1] Wittgenstein, *Tractatus*, 4. 461.

is a strong word, and logicians nowadays are not given to using strong words; a full discussion of its meaning, especially in mathematical contexts, would occupy many pages; but for my present purposes it may be defined accurately enough as follows: A sentence P entails a sentence Q if and only if the fact that a person assents to P but dissents from Q is a sufficient criterion for saying that he has misunderstood one or other of the sentences.[1] 'Sentence' here is an abbreviation for 'sentence as used by a particular speaker on a particular occasion'; for speakers may on different occasions use words with different meanings, and this means that what is entailed by what they say will also differ. We elicit their meaning by asking them what they regard their remarks as entailing.[2]

Now the word 'all' and other logical words are used in commands, as in statements. It follows that there must also be entailment-relations between commands; for otherwise it would be impossible to give any meaning to these words as used in them. If we had to find out whether someone knew the meaning of the word 'all' in 'Take all the boxes to the station', we should have to find out whether he realized that a person who assented to this command, and also to the statement 'This is one of the boxes' and yet refused to assent to the command 'Take this to the station' could only do so if he had misunderstood one of these three sentences. If this sort of test were inapplicable the word 'all' (in imperatives as in indicatives) would be entirely meaningless. We may there-

[1] More complicated entailments, such as those in mathematics, might be covered by extending this definition as follows: the definition given would be treated as a definition of *direct* entailment, and *indirect* entailment would be defined as holding between two sentences P and R when there is a series of sentences $Q_1, Q_2 \ldots Q_n$ such that P directly entails Q_1, Q_1 directly entails Q_2, &c., and Q_n directly entails R. But even this may not be sufficiently exact.

[2] For an indication of how logical symbols may be defined in terms of the entailment-relations of sentences containing them, see K. R. Popper, 'New Foundations for Logic', *Mind*, lvi (1947), 193, and 'Logic without Assumptions', *Aristotelian Society* xlviii (1946–7), 251.

fore say that the existence in our language of universal sentences in the imperative mood is in itself sufficient proof that our language admits of entailments of which at least one term is a command. Whether the word 'entail' is to be used for these relations is only a matter of terminological convenience. I propose so to use it.[1]

I gave, in the article quoted, a number of examples of entailments whose conclusions are commands. It would seem possible in principle, since the ordinary logical words occur in the phrastics of imperatives, to reconstruct the ordinary sentential calculus in terms of phrastics only, and then apply it to indicatives and imperatives alike simply by adding the appropriate neustics.[2] It would remain to be determined to what extent the calculus, as so reconstructed, would correspond to our ordinary language; this is a familiar problem in

---

[1] The reasons why many people have wished to deny that commands can entail or be entailed are mainly historical. But Aristotle speaks of practical as well as theoretical syllogisms (*Movement of Animals*, 701^a 7 ff., *Nicomachean Ethics*, 1144^a 31). He treated the major premiss of the former as a gerundive or a 'should'-sentence or in other ways, but never seems to have realized how different these forms are from normal indicatives. Moreover he says that the conclusion is an action (not an imperative enjoining an action). He finds the principal logical difference between practical and theoretical reasoning not in the prescriptive character of the former (which he recognizes) but in the fact that, having to conclude in an action, it has to refer to contingent particulars, which theoretical syllogisms (for reasons which we should question) are not by him allowed to do (*Nicomachean Ethics*, 1129^b 19 ff., 1140^a 31 ff., 1147^a 2). This led him to assign a logically inferior status to practical inferences, though they are fundamental to his whole ethical theory; and his work on them has been strangely neglected. It is interesting that his general definition of syllogism, though always given in an indicative context, is sometimes (though not always) put in a form which could apply equally to imperatives: 'Syllogism consists in saying, given certain things, something further which follows necessarily from them' (*Sophistical Refutations*, 165^a 1; cf. *Topics*, 100^a 25, *Prior Analytics*, 24^b 18).

[2] An attempt on these lines has already been made by A. Hofstadter and J. C. C. McKinsey, 'On the logic of Imperatives', *Philosophy of Science*, vi (1939), 446 ff.; but see comments by A. Ross, 'Imperatives and Logic', ibid. xi (1944), 30 ff.

the case of indicative logic, and its solution depends on patiently investigating, whether the logical signs in the calculus are bound by the same rules as determine the meanings of the logical words which we use in our normal speech. It might be found that ordinary speech has a number of different rules for the use of the words 'if', 'or', &c., in different contexts; and in particular their use in indicative contexts might differ from their use in imperative contexts. All this is a matter for inquiry; but it does not in the least affect the principle that, provided that we either find out what the rules are, or lay down what they are to be, we can study the logic of imperative sentences with as much assurance as that of indicatives. There can be, here as elsewhere, no question of 'rival logics', but only of alternative rules determining the use (i.e. the entailment-relations) of our logical signs; it is a tautology to say that so long as we continue to use our words in the same sense, their entailment-relations will remain the same.[1]

2. 5. Here we need not go into these complications. We shall need, in this inquiry, to consider only the inference from universal imperative sentences, together with indicative minor premisses, to singular imperative conclusions. I have already given an example of such an inference, and maintained that, if it were impossible to make inferences of this kind, the word 'all' would have no meaning in commands. But this type of inference does raise a further difficulty, because one of the premisses is in the indicative, and one in the imperative. The inference is:

> Take all the boxes to the station.
> This is one of the boxes.
>
> ∴ Take this to the station.

It might be asked how we are to know, given two premisses

[1] For a discussion of possible differences between imperative and indicative logic, see G. H. von Wright, 'Deontic Logic', *Mind*, lx (1951); it is important to realize that *modal* imperative logic is as distinct from the logic of simple imperatives as in the case of the indicative mood.

in different moods, in what mood the conclusion is to be. The problem of the effect upon inferences of the moods of premisses and conclusion has been ignored by logicians who have not looked beyond the indicative mood, though there is no reason why they should have ignored it—for how should we set about demonstrating that the conclusion from a set of indicative premisses must also be in the indicative? But if, as I do, we regard the entailment-relations of ordinary logic as relations between the phrastics of sentences, the problem becomes pressing. Granted that the reason for the validity of the above syllogism is that the phrastics 'Your taking all the boxes to the station and this being one of the boxes' and 'Your not taking this to the station' are logically inconsistent with one another, because of the logical rules governing the use of the word 'all', how are we to know that we cannot add neustics in a different way from the above? We might write, for example:

> Take all the boxes to the station.
> This is one of the boxes.

∴ You are going to take this to the station.

and call this a valid syllogism, which it plainly is not.

Let me first state two of the rules that seem to govern this matter; we may leave till later the question of their justification. The rules are:

(1) *No indicative conclusion can be validly drawn from a set of premisses which cannot be validly drawn from the indicatives among them alone.*
(2) *No imperative conclusion can be validly drawn from a set of premisses which does not contain at least one imperative.*

It is only the second rule which will concern us in this inquiry. There is a very important apparent exception to this rule, the so-called 'hypothetical imperative', with which I shall deal in the next chapter. For the moment, however, let us take the rule as it stands. It is of the most profound im-

portance for ethics. This will be clear if I give a list of some famous arguments in ethics that seem to me to have been wittingly or unwittingly founded upon it. If we admit, as I shall later maintain, that it must be part of the function of a moral judgement to prescribe or guide choices, that is to say, to entail an answer to some question of the form 'What shall I do?'—then it is clear, from the second of the rules just stated, that no moral judgement can be a pure statement of fact. On this foundation rests, indirectly, Socrates' refutation of Cephalus' definition of justice as 'speaking the truth and giving back anything that one has received from anyone', and of all Polemarchus' subsequent modifications of this definition.[1] Aristotle was appealing indirectly to this rule when he made his most decisive break with Platonism, his rejection of the Idea of the Good; he gave, among other reasons, the reason that if there were such an Idea, sentences about it would not be action-guiding ('it would not be a good that you could by your action bring into existence').[2] In the place of a factual, existing good, knowable by a kind of supra-sensible observation, Aristotle puts a 'good to be achieved by action' or, as he usually calls it, an 'end'; that is to say, he implicitly recognizes that, if to say something is good is to guide action, then it cannot be merely to state a fact about the world. Most of his ethical differences from Plato can be traced to this source.

In this logical rule, again, is to be found the basis of Hume's celebrated observation on the impossibility of deducing an 'ought'-proposition from a series of 'is'-propositions—an observation which, as he rightly says, 'would subvert all the vulgar systems of morality', and not only those which had already appeared in his day.[3] Kant, too, rested upon this rule in his polemic against 'Heteronomy of the will

[1] Plato, *Republic*, 331 c ff.
[2] *Nicomachean Ethics*, 1096^b 32.
[3] *Treatise*, iii. 1, i.

as the source of all spurious principles of morality'. There he says 'If the will . . . going beyond itself seeks this law in the character of any of its objects—the result is always heteronomy'.[1] The reason why heteronomous principles of morality are spurious is that from a series of indicative sentences about 'the character of any of its objects' no imperative sentence about what is to be done can be derived, and therefore no moral judgement can be derived from it either.

In more recent times this rule was the point behind Professor G. E. Moore's celebrated 'refutation of naturalism', as we shall later see (11. 3). It was also the point behind Prichard's attack upon Rashdall.[2] Prichard in effect argues that the goodness of a situation (which both he and those he is attacking regard as a fact about the situation) does not by itself constitute a reason why we ought to try to bring that situation into being; we need also what he (somewhat misleadingly) calls 'the feeling of imperativeness or obligation which is to be aroused by the thought of the action which will originate it'. And indeed, if the word 'good' is treated in the fashion that many intuitionists have treated it, this argument is perfectly valid; for sentences containing the word as so understood will not be genuine evaluative judgements, because no imperatives can be derived from them.[3] But this objection applies, not only to the intuitionist theory of 'good', but to all who insist on the solely factual character of moral judgements; it applies to Prichard himself. Professor Ayer[4] uses an argument against intuitionists in general which is based upon this fundamental rule. But in all these cases the appeal to the rule is only implicit. I know only two places in which the rule is explicitly stated; the first is by Poincaré,[5]

[1] *Groundwork of the Metaphysic of Morals*, tr. H. J. Paton, pp. 108 ff.
[2] *Moral Obligation*, p. 4.
[3] For a similar view, cf. W. K. Frankena, in *The Philosophy of G. E. Moore*, ed. P. Schilpp, p. 100.
[4] 'On the Analysis of Moral Judgments', *Philosophical Essays*, p. 240.
[5] *Dernières pensées*, p. 225.

who, however, makes what seems to me an illegitimate use of it, as will be apparent from the preceding argument; the second is by Professor Popper.[1] Popper rightly refers to the rule as 'perhaps the simplest and the most important point about ethics'. A judgement is not moral if it does not provide, without further imperative premisses, a reason for doing something.

[1] 'What can Logic do for Philosophy?', *Aristotelian Society*, Supplementary Vol. xxii (1948), 154; cf. *The Open Society*, ii. 51 ff.

3

INFERENCE

3. 1. THE rule that an imperative cannot appear in the conclusion of a valid inference, unless there is at least one imperative in the premisses, may be confirmed by an appeal to general logical considerations. For it is now generally regarded as true by definition that (to·speak roughly at first) nothing can appear in the conclusion of a valid deductive inference which is not, from their very meaning, implicit in the conjunction of the premisses. It follows that, if there is an imperative in the conclusion, not only must *some* imperative appear in the premisses, but that very imperative must be itself implicit in them.

Since these considerations have a wide bearing on moral philosophy, it will be as well to explain them in greater detail. Few people now think, as Descartes seems to have done, that we can arrive at scientific conclusions about matters of empirical fact, like the circulation of the blood, by deductive reasoning from self-evident first principles.[1] The work of Wittgenstein and others has to a great extent made clear the reasons for the impossibility of doing this. It has been argued, convincingly in my opinion, that all deductive inference is analytic in character; that is to say, that the function of a deductive inference is not to get from the premisses 'something further' not implicit in them (even if that is what Aristotle meant (2. 4)), but to make explicit what was implicit in the conjunction of the premisses. This has been shown to follow from the very nature of language; for to say anything we have, as we have already noticed, to obey some rules, and these rules—especially but not only the rules for the use of the so-called logical words—mean, firstly, that to say what is

[1] Cf. *Discourse on Method*, Part V.

in the premisses of a valid inference is to say, at least, what is in the conclusion, and, secondly, that if anything is said in the conclusion which is not said, implicitly or explicitly, in the premisses, the inference is invalid. We cannot be said to understand fully the meaning of premisses and conclusion unless we admit the validity of the inference. Thus, if someone professed to admit that all men were mortal and that Socrates was a man, but refused to admit that Socrates was mortal, the correct thing to do would be not, as has sometimes been suggested, to accuse him of some kind of logical purblindness, but to say 'You evidently don't know the meaning of the word "all"; for if you did you would *eo ipso* know how to make inferences of this sort'.

3. 2. The principle just set out is not, however, quite general enough to cover all cases. For example, '$x = 2$' entails '$x^2 = 4$'; but it is not natural to say that in the latter expression nothing is said which is not said implicitly in the former; for the latter contains the 'squared' symbol, and in order to understand '$x = 2$' we do not have to know anything about the meaning of this symbol. We have, therefore, to say that there must be nothing said in the conclusion which is not said implicitly or explicitly in the premisses, *except what can be added solely on the strength of definitions of terms*. This qualification is important for the logic of imperatives; for, as I have already warned the reader, there is one kind of imperative conclusion which can be entailed by a set of purely indicative premisses. This is the so-called 'hypothetical' imperative. It must be pointed out that not all imperatives containing a hypothetical clause are 'hypothetical' in this sense. For example, the sentence 'If any statement is untrue, do not make it', is not 'hypothetical' as the expression 'hypothetical imperative' is traditionally used. What a 'hypothetical' imperative is, is best made clear by examples. The subject is so difficult that I cannot deal with it very fully; but some explanation is necessary.

Consider the following sentence:

If you want to go to the largest grocer in Oxford, go to Grimbly Hughes.

This seems to follow from, and to say no more than:

Grimbly Hughes is the largest grocer in Oxford.

The first matter that requires elucidation is the status of the word 'want'. It does not mean the same as 'be affected by a recognizable state of the feelings known as desire'. If I were the superior of a religious order whose rule ordained the complete abnegation of all desires, I could not say to a novice 'If you have a desire to go to the largest grocer in Oxford, go to Grimbly Hughes', for this would be contrary to the rule. But I might very well say 'If you want to go to the largest grocer in Oxford, go to Grimbly Hughes'; for this would simply be intended to convey a piece of information that the largest grocer is Grimbly Hughes. 'Want' is here a logical term, and stands, as we shall see, for an imperative inside a subordinate clause. This is but one of the many puzzles generated by treating sentences compounded with the word 'want' as if they were always descriptive of mental states (1. 3).

Now compare the following sentence:

If all mules are barren, then this animal is barren.

This is entailed by the sentence 'This animal is a mule'. We only have to know the meanings of 'all' and the other words used in order to make the inference. We must notice that this inference is valid because another simpler one is valid, namely:

> All mules are barren.
> This animal is a mule.
>
> ∴ This animal is barren.

The more complex form of the inference is arrived at by taking away the major premiss from its proper place, and adding it to the conclusion inside an hypothetical clause.

The following inference can also be treated in the same way:

Go to the largest grocer in Oxford.
Grimbly Hughes is the largest grocer in Oxford.

∴ Go to Grimbly Hughes.

It then becomes:

Grimbly Hughes is the largest grocer in Oxford.

∴ If go to the largest grocer in Oxford, go to Grimbly Hughes.

In English, we write this conclusion in the form:

If you want to go to the largest grocer in Oxford, go to Grimbly Hughes.

We only have to know the meanings of 'want' and the other words used in the conclusion (including the imperative verb-form) in order to make this inference.

Another example would be 'If you want to break your springs, go on driving as you are at the moment'. Here the full inference would be:

Do whatever will conduce to breaking your springs.
Going on driving as you are at the moment will conduce, &c.

∴ Go on driving as you are at the moment.

The speaker of our example, in order to draw the hearer's attention in an emphatic way to the truth of the minor premiss, points out that his present style of driving would be a valid conclusion from this minor premiss and a major premiss which the hearer obviously does not accept. Into this example, the notion of 'means conducive to an end' enters; but the first example shows that it need not be present.

Other related forms of expression are:

To stop the train pull down the chain.
Drive slowly or you'll have a collision.
Omit regular lubrication and halve the life of your car.

There is a marked contrast between these three; the first is neutral on the subject of whether the chain is actually to be pulled or not; that is why 'Penalty for improper use £5' has to be added. The second is not neutral; it has a strong flavour of the simple, non-hypothetical imperative 'Drive slowly', and 'or' might be replaced by 'because if you don't'. The third is an oddity; like 'If you want to break your springs, go on driving as you are at the moment', it is ironic and actually has the purpose of dissenting from the clause 'Omit regular lubrication'. It is adapted, with the omission of a trade name, from an actual advertisement.

To the extent that an imperative is hypothetical, it has descriptive force in much the same way as a value-judgement may (7. 1). Understanding or supplying the hypothetical clause is like knowing the standard of values that is being applied. It is not easy to say, in any individual case, in which there is no 'if'-clause actually included, to what extent the imperative is to be treated as hypothetical. We must not assume that all non-moral imperatives are hypothetical, for this is far from being true. Operating instructions for machinery form an interesting borderline case. Are we to say that 'Plug in to a supply of the voltage indicated on the label' is hypothetical, and that we have to understand 'if you want your vacuum cleaner to clean your carpets without necessitating expensive repairs'? It is hard to answer this question; we could certainly understand and obey the instruction without knowing what its purpose was. This case shows, not that there is no difference between hypothetical and non-hypothetical imperatives, but that the line is hard to draw.

It would probably be misleading to say that hypothetical imperatives are 'really indicatives'. They have indeed descriptive force, and are entailed by indicatives; but '$x^2 = 4$' is entailed by '$x = 2$', and yet we should not say that the former was not really a quadratic equation. It would not, for one thing, be intelligible to someone who did not know the meaning of the 'squared' symbol. This symbol, moreover, does not have here a special meaning different from its other uses. In somewhat the same way, 'If you want to go to the largest grocer in Oxford, go to Grimbly Hughes' is not an indicative; it would not be intelligible to someone who had learnt the meaning of indicative verb-forms but not that of imperative verb-forms; and the latter do not have in it a special meaning. The best way of describing the matter has been suggested by Kant: the imperative element in a hypothetical imperative is analytic ('Who wills the end . . . wills also the means'), because the imperatives in the two parts, so to say, cancel one another out. It is an imperative, but, *qua* imperative, has no content; the content which it has is that of the indicative minor premiss from which it is derived.[1]

Two suggestions may be made for further researches into the subject of hypothetical imperatives which cannot be pursued here. The first is that the 'if' in them has a somewhat different logical status from that which it has in sentences like 'If any statement is untrue, do not make it'. If the latter sentence were analysed into phrastic and neustic, it seems to me that the 'if' would go into the phrastic; the whole sentence might be rendered thus:

In the event of any statement being untrue, your not making it, please,

or thus:

Your not making untrue statements, please.

But in a hypothetical imperative proper the 'if'-clause itself contains an imperative neustic, concealed in the word 'want'. I am not sure yet how these sentences would be best analysed, and am inclined to think that different ones should be analysed in different ways according to how fully 'hypothetical' they are. If the categorical element is completely submerged, as

---

[1] *Groundwork of the Metaphysic of Morals*, tr. H. J. Paton, pp. 84–85.

in 'If you want to break your springs, go on driving as you are at present', a metalinguistic analysis is tempting:

The command 'Go on driving as you are at present' could be inferred from a minor factual premiss, which is true, and the major premiss (*sc.* to which you obviously do not assent) 'Do whatever will conduce to breaking your springs'.

But this problem is part of the wider problem, still very dark, of the analysis of hypothetical sentences in general.

The second suggestion is, that the relation between hypothetical imperatives and the descriptive element in the meaning of value-judgements would repay much further study. The suggestion just made, that some hypothetical imperatives might be analysed metalinguistically, clearly has a bearing on what I shall later call the 'inverted-commas' use of value-judgements (7. 5). It may safely be predicted that hypothetical imperatives will be found to be as subtle, flexible, and various in their logic as are the descriptive uses of value-words.

3. 3. But let us leave this difficult matter and return to Descartes. The considerations about inference which I summarized at the beginning of this chapter mean that a Cartesian procedure, either in science or in morals, is doomed from the very start. If any science is intended to give us conclusions of substance about matters of fact, then, if its method is deductive, these conclusions must be implicit in the premisses. This means that, before we fully understand the meanings of our Cartesian first principles, we have to know that they (with the addition only of definitions of terms) entail such various propositions as, that all mules are barren, or that a man's heart is on the left-hand side of his body, or that the sun is so many miles from the earth. But if all these facts are implicit in the first principles, the latter can hardly be called self-evident. We find out about facts like these at least in part by observation; no amount of reasoning from

axioms will take its place. The position of pure mathematics
has been much discussed and is still obscure; it seems best
to regard the axioms of pure mathematics and logic as
definitive of the terms used in them. But this much, at any
rate, may be said, that if a science purports to tell us facts like
the above, it cannot, like pure mathematics, be based on deductive reasoning and nothing else. It was the mistake of
Descartes to assimilate to pure mathematics studies which are
of a wholly different character.

It does not follow, from the fact that deduction, whether
in the form of pure mathematics or of logic, cannot take the
place of observation, that deduction is therefore altogether
useless as an adjunct to observation. Science makes use of
expressions which would be altogether meaningless unless we
could deduce. The sentence 'There are three gramme weights
on the balance and no more' would be meaningless to anyone
who could not deduce from it 'There is one gramme weight
on the balance, and one other, and one other, and no more',
and vice versa.

The same considerations hold good in ethics. Many of the
ethical theories which have been proposed in the past may
without injustice be called 'Cartesian' in character; that is to
say, they try to deduce particular duties from some self-
evident first principle. Often factual observations are admitted among the premisses; but this, though it makes the
theories which admit them incompletely 'Cartesian', does not
affect my argument. A Cartesian procedure in morals is as
illusory as it is in science. If we may take it that, as I shall
show later, a piece of genuinely evaluative moral reasoning
must have as its end-product an imperative of the form 'Do
so-and-so', it follows that its principles must be of such a kind
that we can deduce such particular imperatives from them,
in conjunction with factual minor premisses. If, for example,
a moral system is to enjoin me not to say this particular thing
which is false, its principles must contain implicitly or

explicitly an imperative to the effect that what is false is not to be said in circumstances like those in which I now am. And, similarly, they must contain other imperatives such as will regulate my conduct in all manner of circumstances, both foreseen and unforeseen. But it is obvious that such a set of principles could not possibly be self-evident. It is not easier, but more difficult, to assent to a very general command like 'Never say what is false' than it is to assent to the particular command 'Do not say this particular thing which is false', just as it is more difficult and dangerous to adopt the hypothesis that all mules are barren than to acknowledge the undoubted fact that this mule which has just died has had no progeny. A decision never to say what is false involves a decision in advance about a very great number of individual cases, with only the information about them that they are all cases of saying what is false. It is not, surely, casuistry of an objectionable kind to want to avoid committing ourselves in this fashion. It is quite true that, when we have had experience of making such decisions, we may eventually find ourselves able to accept the general principle. But suppose that we were faced, for the first time, with the question 'Shall I now say what is false?' and had no past decisions, either of our own or of other people, to guide us. How should we then decide the question? Not, surely, by inference from a self-evident general principle, 'Never say what is false'; for if we could not decide even whether to say what was false in these particular circumstances, how could we possibly decide whether to say what was false in innumerable circumstances whose details were totally unknown to us, save in this respect, that they were all cases of saying what was false?

The same point may be put in another way. It is an established principle of logic that if one proposition entails another, then the negation of the second entails the negation of the first. An analogous principle, somewhat stronger, is also valid, that if I know that one proposition entails another, to be in doubt about assenting to the second is *eo ipso* to be in doubt about assenting to the first. For instance, if I know that the proposition 'All mules are barren and this is a mule' entails the proposition 'This (mule) is barren', it follows that if I am in doubt about assenting to the proposition 'This (mule) is barren', I must be in doubt about assenting to the proposition 'All mules are barren and this is a mule'; and this means that I must be in doubt about either 'All mules are barren' or 'This is a mule'. Now if we apply an exactly parallel reasoning to our case about saying what is false, we get the following result. Since I am in doubt, *ex hypothesi*, whether or not to make this false statement, I must be in doubt about assenting to the command 'Do not make this statement'. But if I am in doubt about this command, I must *eo ipso* be in doubt, either about the factual premiss 'This statement is false' (and this alternative is ruled out *ex hypothesi*), or else, as must be the case, about the imperative premiss 'Never say what is false'. It follows that no general principle can be self-evident which is to be of assistance in deciding particular questions about which we are in doubt.

The impossibility of a 'Cartesian' moral system may be shown in another way, closely akin to the one just explained. It is not in the least clear what could be meant by calling any proposition, least of all a general principle of conduct, 'self-evident'. If such a principle is to be in some sense impossible to reject, this, it seems to me, can only be for one of two reasons. First, it might be said that a principle of conduct was impossible to reject, if it were *self-contradictory* to reject it. But if it is self-contradictory to reject a principle, this can only be because the principle is analytic. But if it is analytic, it cannot have any content; it cannot tell me to do one thing rather than another. The term 'analytic', which we shall have occasion to use a good deal, may be defined with sufficient precision as follows: A sentence is analytic if, and only if, either (1) the fact that a person dissents from it is a sufficient criterion for saying that he has misunderstood the speaker's meaning or (2) it is entailed by some sentence which is analytic in sense (1). A sentence which is not analytic or self-contradictory is called synthetic. These definitions are of course not exact; a full discussion of the meanings of 'analytic' and 'synthetic' is outside the scope of this book.

Secondly, it might be suggested that a principle of conduct might be impossible to reject, in the sense that its rejection was a psychological impossibility. But what is or is not a psychological impossibility is a contingent matter; it may be a psychological impossibility for *me* to reject a principle which the more hardened or sophisticated have no difficulty in discarding. We could never have any justification for asserting that no one could ever reject a principle, unless that principle were analytic. Moreover, the psychological impossibility of rejecting a principle would be a fact about the constitution of people's psyches; and from a fact, or the indicative sentence recording it, no imperative can be derived.

A third kind of interpretation is sometimes canvassed, which rests upon the introduction of a value-word. It might be suggested that, though a principle was both logically and psychologically possible to reject, it might be not *rational* to reject it (it might be impossible for a rational person to reject it). Sometimes instead of 'rational' we have other expressions, such as 'a morally developed or morally educated person' or 'a competent and impartial judge'. These are all value-expressions. We therefore have to ask 'What could be the criterion for deciding whether a person falls into one or other of these classes?' Clearly we cannot say that the rejection of the principle is itself evidence that the person who rejects it is not qualified in these ways; for in this case our criterion of self-evidence would be circular. There must therefore be some other means of finding out whether a person is rational. But the question whether a person is rational must be either a factual question or a question of value (or a combination of the two). If it is a purely factual question, then we cannot get imperative conclusions out of factual premisses such as 'So-and-so is rational' and 'So-and-so finds it impossible to reject the principle that . . .'. But if it is wholly or partly a question of value, then either the answer to it is self-evident in some sense (in which case again our criterion of self-evidence would be circular), or else we have at least one constituent in our reasoning which is neither factual nor self-evident. This third possibility, therefore, must be ruled out.

It follows from these considerations that if it is the function of general moral principles to regulate our conduct, i.e. to entail, in conjunction with indicative minor premisses, answers to questions of the form 'Shall I or shall I not do this particular thing?' then these general moral principles cannot be self-evident. If this view of the function of moral principles were accepted (and I shall later give reasons for doing so), it would provide a conclusive refutation of a large number of ethical theories. Suppose, for example, that we find a philosopher telling us that it is self-evident that we ought always to do what our conscience tells us; we must answer that, since we are often in doubt whether or not to do some act which our conscience tells us to do, this general principle cannot be self-evident. And even if it were the case that we never were in doubt on this point, this would be merely a fact about our psyches, and no imperative conclusions would follow from it. In the example chosen, 'conscience' must, of course, be taken as the name of an identifiable psychological occurrence. If it is made a value-question, whether a certain psychological occurrence is really conscience or the Devil assuming the voice of conscience, the principle clearly comes within the scope of the next paragraph.

Ethical theories of this general type usually conceal their fallacious character by a device of which a brief mention may be made here, although it cannot be fully understood until we have discussed the logic of value-words. If the general principle advocated contains a value-word, it may be made to appear self-evident, by being treated as analytic; and then, when the same value-word appears in the factual minor premiss, it may be treated as if it were descriptive. For example, we might assert the self-evidence (because analytic) of the principle that we ought to do our duty; and then we might argue that we could ascertain what our duty was by some fact-finding process (e.g. by consulting a faculty called a sense of duty, or else by seeing to what kinds of act the word 'duty' was applied in our society, and then calling these acts 'duties'). From this argument it would appear that we could get to a conclusion 'I ought to do a particular act A' and thence to the imperative 'Do A', simply on the basis of two premisses 'One ought to do one's duty' and 'A is my duty', the first of which is self-evident and the second factual. But this is an equivocation. If 'duty' is a value-word, then we cannot decide what is our duty merely by consulting word-usage or by seeing whether we have a certain psychological reaction, but only by making a moral decision. On the other hand, if 'duty' were not treated as a value-word, but regarded as meaning either 'that towards which I have a certain recognizable psychological reaction' or 'that to which the name "duty" is commonly applied in my society', then the principle 'One ought always to do one's duty' would not be self-evident.

3. 4. The upshot of all this is rather alarming. I gave in the preceding chapter reasons for holding that no moral system whose principles were regarded as purely factual could fulfil its function of regulating our conduct. In this chapter I have shown that no moral system which claims to be based on principles which are self-evident can fulfil this function either. These two contentions between them, if they are accepted, dispose of nearly all of what Hume calls 'the vulgar systems of morality'. Most ethical writers who have seemed plausible to those who studied them superficially, can be shown to suffer from one or other of these defects. A few great writers, such as Aristotle, Hume, and Kant, though it is not difficult to find here and there in their works traces of these defects, can yet, if studied in the right way, be seen to avoid them in their main doctrines. But it is not surprising that the first effect of modern logical researches was to make some philosophers despair of morals as a rational activity.

It is the purpose of this book to show that their despair was premature. But the effects of the above argument are so catastrophic that it may well be asked 'Have you not from the start rendered the problem impossible of solution? Is there not some flaw in your argument, some dichotomy too stringently pressed, some criterion interpreted too exactly; can we not save something from the destruction by being a little less rigorous?' In particular, exception will certainly be taken to my use of the word 'entail'. It may be maintained that although, in the strict sense of the word, I have indeed shown that moral judgements and imperatives cannot be *entailed* by factual premisses, yet there is some looser relation than entailment which holds between them. Mr. S. E. Toulmin, for example, talks of:

an ethical argument, consisting partly of logical (demonstrative) inferences, partly of scientific (inductive) inferences, and partly of that form of inference peculiar to ethical arguments, by which we pass from factual reasons to an ethical conclusion—what we may naturally call 'evaluative' inference.[1]

Since I have elsewhere, in a review of Toulmin's book,[2] discussed his particular version of this doctrine, which avoids the crudest of the errors to which I shall be calling attention, I shall content myself here with some general remarks about this kind of approach to the problem.

---

[1] *Reason in Ethics*, p. 38.
[2] *Philosophical Quarterly*, i (1951), 372.

Let us first glance at the history of this type of theory. It is, I think, clear that its immediate origins are to be found in the attack by writers of the verificationist school upon ethics as a branch of philosophy. The theory is intended to save ethics from this attack by showing that moral judgements are, after all, good empirical propositions, only their method of verification is different from, and somewhat looser than, that of ordinary fact-stating sentences. Thus they are indeed inferrable from observations of fact, but in a looser way.

Now this programme is from the start misconceived. A statement, however loosely it is bound to the facts, cannot answer a question of the form 'What shall I do?'; only a command can do this. Therefore, if we insist that moral judgements are nothing but loose statements of fact, we preclude them from fulfilling their main function; for their main function is to regulate conduct, and they can do this only if they are interpreted in such a way as to have imperative or prescriptive force. Since I am not concerned here with moral judgements as such, I shall leave till later the question 'How is the prescriptive force of moral judgements related to the descriptive function which they also normally have?' I am concerned here with the more fundamental problem of what sorts of reasoning can have as their end-product answers to questions of the form 'What shall I do?' It is clear that until we have clarified this more fundamental problem, we shall not be able to say much about the prescriptive force of moral judgements. Here it will suffice to show why, although prescription and description may be combined in the same judgement, description is not and never can be prescription. In other words, I am going to give reasons for holding that by no form of inference, however loose, can we get an answer to the question 'What shall I do?' out of a set of premises which do not contain, at any rate implicitly, an imperative.

3. 5. My reasons for holding this are three. First, to hold that an imperative conclusion can be derived from purely

indicative premisses leads to representing matters of substance as if they were verbal matters. In this connexion it is
interesting to recall the parallel mistake of Professor Carnap
in regard to physical laws. Carnap once held that, by the in-
clusion of suitable rules of inference in what he called the
P-language (i.e. the language of a science) the statements of
the science could be shown to be true in virtue of their form
alone; and to say this is to assimilate those statements to what
are normally called analytic statements—though Carnap himself calls them synthetic, using the word in a special sense.[1]
This may seem a neat way of showing how scientific truths
can be said to be necessary, and thus solving the troublesome
'problem of induction'. But if we ask 'What are these special
rules of inference?' it is bound to appear that they are nothing
but the laws of the science in another guise. Thus, if we have
a rule of inference to the effect that we can proceed from 'This
is a mule' to 'This (mule) is barren', then obviously our rule
of inference only states in a new way the old law 'All mules
are barren'. The question then arises, 'Is it proper to treat a
law of science as if it were a rule of inference?' It is natural
to say that it is not; for, as the work of Professor Popper,
already referred to, has made clear, the rules of inference of
ordinary logic can be shown to depend on the definitions of
the logical words (2. 4, note). Thus, for example, it is part
of the meaning of the word 'all' that we can infer from 'All
mules are barren and this is a mule' the sentence 'This (mule)
is barren'. If, therefore, we want to assimilate the laws of
science to rules of inference, we shall have to show that they,
likewise, follow from the meanings of the words used; for
example, we shall have to show that the reason why we can
pass from 'This is a mule' to 'This (mule) is barren' has something to do with the meaning of the words 'mule' and 'barren'.
But to say this is to be guilty of conventionalism, the defects
of which have been shown by the work (among others) of

[1] *Logical Syntax of Language*, pp. 184–5.

Professor von Wright.[1] The sentence 'All mules are barren' tells us something, not about words, but about the world; and therefore it cannot be treated as a definition, nor as something analogous to a logical rule of inference. The only kind of definition to which it is in the least similar is an Aristotelian 'real' definition, or part of one, to the effect that it is—in fact—a property of mules that they are barren; unlikely as the conventionalists would be to admit it, their definitions and rules of inference have to be treated as 'real' in this sense if they are to do the job required of them.

The position with regard to conduct is similar. The view which I am attacking holds that by having special rules of inference we can say that there can be inferences from a set of indicative premisses to an imperative conclusion. If we ask 'What are these special rules of inference?' it is clear that they are nothing but the old rules of conduct in a new guise. What under the old dispensation appears as an imperative major premiss reappears under the new as a rule of inference. The criterion which I suggest for deciding on the merits of these two ways of putting the matter is the same as before. Let us take an example. Suppose that I say 'Don't say that, because it is false'. Are we to represent this argument as follows:

S is false.

∴ Do not say S,

or shall we add the imperative major premiss 'Never say what is false'? If the latter, the inference is valid by the ordinary rules of logic; but if the former, we have to have a special rule of inference, which will just be this imperative major premiss in another capacity. Does it matter which of these alternatives we choose? Surely it does if we are concerned to distinguish between on the one hand general principles about our conduct, which have content, and tell us to do, or to

[1] *Logical Problem of Induction*, ch. iii.

refrain from, certain positive acts in our external behaviour, and on the other logical rules, which are rules, not for behaving correctly, but for talking and thinking correctly, and are, if Popper is to be believed, not about our actions, but about the meanings of the words used.

This argument would tell equally against a theory which reduced rules of conduct to definitions of value-words; for in that case also arguments about how one should behave would turn into merely verbal disputes. Suppose that a Communist and I are arguing about whether I ought to do a certain act A; and suppose that on his principles I ought not to do it, whereas on mine I ought. An advocate of the sort of theory that I am attacking might treat this dispute as follows: each of the disputants has his own way of verifying the sentence 'I ought in these circumstances to do A'; and these ways differ. Therefore, in order to avoid such disputes, it would be better for us to substitute two unambiguous terms for the one ambiguous one; for example, the Communist should use the term 'ought$_1$' for the concept governed by his rules of verification, and I should use 'ought$_2$' for *my* concept. But the point is that there *is* a dispute, and not merely a verbal misunderstanding, between the Communist and me; we are differing about what I ought to *do* (not *say*) and, if he convinces me, my conduct will be substantially different from what it would be if I remained unconvinced.

3. 6. My second reason for objecting to this kind of approach is that, if one is going to introduce looseness into our talk about conduct, it is as well to make clear in just what this looseness consists; and I am myself far from clear what is being proposed. Let us admit for the sake of argument that we are at liberty, if we please, to treat principles like 'Never say what is false' as rules of inference; we have then to ask, in what respect these rules of inference differ from the ordinary rules of logic. I have already given my own answer, that they differ in the same way as scientific laws differ from rules of logic, because they are about matters of substance, not about words—though in this case the matters of substance are not matters of fact, but of what we should do. The answer given by the type of theory which I am criticizing is, that these rules of inference are *looser* than the rules of logic. Thus, if I say 'This is false, but say it', I am not *contradicting* myself, but only breaking the looser rule to the effect that the inference

S is false.

∴ Do not say S.

is 'in general' valid. It could be argued in favour of this way of treating the matter that we do often say 'Don't say S, because it's false', which presumably rests upon an inference like that just set out; but that this cannot be a strict entailment, because I would not ordinarily be said to contradict myself if I said 'S is false, but say it'.

We have therefore to inquire what can be meant by saying that a rule is 'in general' valid, but not universally. It sounds sensible to say that the rule 'Never say what is false' is a rule of this sort; for in fact we do think it right to observe it in the majority of cases, but we also think it right to break it in exceptional cases in the interests, for example, of tact, the winning of wars, or the preservation of innocent people from homicidal maniacs. Now I can think of at least two ways in which a rule or principle can be incompletely rigorous. The first way is when the rule lays down that a certain kind of action is in certain circumstances to be done, but it is understood that it is sufficient if it is done in the great majority of instances; exceptions are allowed if they are not too numerous in proportion to the total number of cases. An example of such a principle would be the principle that undergraduates must not take a week off work during term; clearly if once or twice during his career an undergraduate, whose industry is otherwise exemplary, takes some time off, even a week, we think no harm of it; but if he takes every week off, or even the majority, he probably gets into serious trouble. It is clear that the principle about not saying what is false is not of this character, because we do not say 'It doesn't matter your saying what is false occasionally, so long as you don't do it too often'.

The distinguishing character of this first kind of loose principle is that the exceptions to it are limited solely in number, and not otherwise determined. Provided that the undergraduate does not take time off constantly it does not matter whether he chooses one week in which to do it rather than another. Thus it is left to his own decision when, if at all, the exceptions to the principle are to be made, provided that they are not numerous. Moreover, his decision to take this week off rather than that effects no modification in the principle; it does not establish a new precedent for idleness that was not there before. Thus we may say that the principle is, *vis-à-vis* its exceptions, static.

Very different is the case with the other kind of 'loose' principle, to which 'Never say what is false' belongs. Here the exceptions are not limited by a numerical restriction, but by the peculiarities of particular classes of instances. We do not say 'Speak the truth in general, but it doesn't matter if you say what is false once in a way'; we say rather 'Speak the truth in general, but there are certain *classes* of cases in which this principle does not hold; for example, you may say what is false in order to save life, and there are other exceptions which you must learn to recognize'. This type of principle is quite different from the first. It is true that here too the decision is left to the agent in the individual case; he has to decide whether to make an exception or not; but what he is deciding is very different. The undergraduate deciding whether to take some time off has not to ask himself whether this is a case of a class which ought to be treated as exceptional. To the first kind of principle, there are not classes of exceptional cases, there are just exceptions, differing in no significant particular from the cases in which the principle is observed. But in the case of the principle 'Do not say what is false', in deciding whether or not to make an exception, we have to think, not 'Have I been breaking this principle much lately?', but 'Is there anything about this case that makes it different from the general run of cases, in such a way that I ought to put cases like it into a special class, and treat them as exceptions?' Thus, with rules of this kind, even exceptions are what I shall be calling decisions of principle, because in making them we are in effect modifying the principle. There is a dynamic relationship between the exceptions and the principle.

This makes it apparent that if we talk about the second kind of principle as being loose, we are being seriously misleading. Looseness in conduct is generally reckoned a bad thing, and it would be dangerous if philosophers were to put about the idea that principles of conduct are loose; for the ordinary person cannot be expected to distinguish readily in what sense they are being called loose. He will naturally take it that they are like the first kind of principle, and that because they are loose he need not trouble to observe them always, provided that he does it often enough to keep up appearances. But in this sense our principles of conduct, as indeed most principles of skill also, are not loose at all. The fact that exceptions are made to them is a sign, not of any essential looseness, but of our desire to make them as rigorous as we can. For what we are doing in allowing classes of exceptions is to make the principle, not looser, but more rigorous. Suppose that we start off with a principle never to say what is false, but regard this principle as provisional, and recognize that there may be exceptions. Suppose, then, that we decide to make an exception in the case of lies told in war-time to deceive the enemy. The rule has now become 'Never say what is false, except in war-time to deceive the enemy'. This principle, once the exception has been made explicit and included in the wording of the principle, is not looser than it was before, but tighter. In one large class of cases, where previously the possibility of exceptions was left open and we had to decide for ourselves, the position is now regulated; the principle lays down that in these circumstances we may say what is false.

This simplified statement of the way in which we modify principles by admitting classes of exceptions covers only those cases where the principle itself is stated in words which leave no doubt as to how to recognize the cases which fall under it. 'Never say what is false' is an example of such a principle. Often, however, principles are stated in such a way as makes it impossible to treat the question, whether a case falls under them, as a mere question of fact. Often, though not always, this is because the principle itself contains, in addition to such imperative verbs or value-words as are necessary for stating a principle of action, other value-words occupying the place that in a normal case would be occupied by purely descriptive terms. For example, we might put our principle about falsehood in a different way: 'Do not tell *lies*.' We might subsequently admit an exception in the case of false-hoods told, not with the intention of deceiving, but for other purposes, for example in order to amuse. Then we might say that to tell a story about someone, which everyone knows is *ben trovato*, is not *lying*. We can say this, because 'lying' does not mean simply telling falsehoods, but telling falsehoods which are *reprehensible*. Thus we might, and sometimes do, make a distinction between lies proper and white lies; lies proper are all reprehensible; a white lie on the other hand is, in the words of the *Oxford English Dictionary*, 'a consciously untrue statement which is not considered criminal: a false-hood rendered venial or praiseworthy by its motive'. In all such cases, the modification of the principle takes the form of an alteration, not of its actual wording, but of the con-ditions under which the principle is held to apply, that is, an alteration of the extension of the crucial word, or as we shall later call it its descriptive meaning, with the retention of its evaluative meaning. This, as has been pointed out to me by Professor H. L. A. Hart, is how legal principles are often modified by judicial decisions, as, for example, by the decision whether or not the occasional cricket ball landing in a public street is properly to be called a 'nuisance'. The word in question need not be (as here) a value-word; it may be a descriptive word whose meaning is loose enough to admit of such treatment. Such decisions, of course, render the law more precise, not looser. The extension of the word may be actually altered, or it may merely be rendered more precise. And it should not need pointing out that decisions of this kind are decisions, and not, as Aristotle seems sometimes to think, exercises of a peculiar kind of perception.[1] We *perceive*, indeed, a difference in the class of case; but we *decide* whether this difference justifies us treating it as exceptional.

Thus, far from principles like 'Never say what is false' being in some way by nature irredeemably loose, it is part of our moral development to turn them from provisional principles into precise principles with their exceptions definitely laid down; this process is, of course, never completed, but it is always going on in any individual lifetime. If we accept and continue to accept such a principle we cannot, as in the case of the rule about taking time off work, break it and leave the principle intact; we have to decide whether to observe the principle and refuse to modify it, or to break it and modify it by admitting a class of exceptions; whereas if the principle were really by nature loose, we could break it without modifying it at all. In the following chapter I shall consider in greater detail how we develop and modify our principles.

3. 7. The gravest error, however, of the type of theory which I am criticizing is that it leaves out of our reasoning about conduct a factor which is of the very essence of morals.

---

[1] *Nicomachean Ethics*, 1109^{b}23, cf. 1126^{b}4.

This factor is decision. In both the kinds of principle which I have been discussing, the principle falls short, in some sense, of being universal, only because in particular cases it is left to the decision of the agent whether to act upon the principle or not. Now to use the word 'inference' of a procedure like this is seriously misleading. When someone says, either 'This is false, so I won't say it', or 'This is false, but I'll say it all the same, and make an exception to my principle', he is doing a lot more than inferring. A process of inference alone would not tell him which of these two things he was to say in any single case falling under the principle. He has to decide which of them to say. Inferring consists in saying that if he tells a falsehood he will be breaking the principle, whereas if he tells the truth he will be observing it. This is a perfectly good deductive inference, and nothing further need be said about it. The rest of what he does is not inference at all, but something quite different, namely, deciding whether to alter the principle or not.

Thus I see no reason to take back what I have said about the way in which principles of conduct entail particular commands. The entailment is rigorous. What we have to investigate is, not some looseness in the entailment, but the way in which we form and modify our principles, and the relation between this process and the particular decisions that we make in the course of it.

4

DECISIONS OF PRINCIPLE

4. 1. THERE are two factors which may be involved in the making of any decision to do something. Of these, the first may at any rate theoretically be absent, the second is always present to some degree. They correspond to the major and minor premisses of the Aristotelian practical syllogism. The major premiss is a principle of conduct; the minor premiss is a statement, more or less full, of what we should in fact be doing if we did one or other of the alternatives open to us. Thus if I decide not to say something, because it is false, I am acting on a principle, 'Never (or never under certain conditions) say what is false', and I must know that this, which I am wondering whether to say, is false.

Let us take the minor premiss first, since it presents less difficulty. We plainly cannot decide what to do unless we know at least something about what we should be doing if we did this or that. For example, suppose that I am an employer, and am wondering whether or not to sack a clerk who habitually turns up at the office after the hour at which he has undertaken to turn up. If I sack him I shall be depriving his family of the money on which they live, perhaps giving my firm a reputation which will lead clerks to avoid it when other jobs are available, and so on; if I keep him, I shall be causing the other clerks to do work which otherwise would be done by this clerk; and the affairs of the office will not be transacted so quickly as they would if all the clerks were punctual. These would be the sorts of consideration that I should take into account in making my decision. They would be the effects on the total situation of the alternative actions, sacking him or not sacking him. It is the effects which determine what I should be doing; it is between the two sets of effects that I am deciding. The whole point about a decision is that it makes a difference to what happens; and this difference is the difference between the effects of deciding one way, and the effects of deciding the other.

It sometimes seems to be implied by writers on ethics that it is immoral, on certain sorts of occasion, to consider the effects of doing something. We ought, it is said, to do our duty no matter what the effects of doing it. As I am using the word 'effects', this cannot be maintained. I am not making a claim for 'expediency' (in the bad sense) as against 'duty'. Even to do our duty—in so far as it is *doing* something—is effecting certain changes in the total situation. It is quite true that, of the changes that it is possible to effect in the total situation, most people would agree that we ought to consider certain kinds more relevant than others (which than which, it is the purpose of moral principles to tell us). I do not think that the immediacy or remoteness of the effects makes any difference, though their certainty or uncertainty does. The reason why it is considered immoral to fail to right an injustice whose effects will maximize pleasure, is not that in such a choice the effects are considered when they should not have been; it is that certain of the effects—namely, the maximization of pleasure—are given a relevance which they should not have, in view of the prior claim of those other effects which would have consisted in the righting of the injustice.

For reasons which will become apparent when we have examined the logic of value-words, it is most important, in a verbal exposition of an argument about what to do, not to allow value-words in the minor premiss. In setting out the facts of the case, we should be as factual as we can. Those versed in the logic of these words, and therefore forewarned against its pitfalls, may in the interests of brevity neglect this precaution; but for the inexperienced it is very much better to keep value-expressions where they belong, in the major premiss. This will prevent the inadvertent admission of an ambiguous middle term, as in the example in 3. 3 *sub fine*. I do not mean that in discussing the facts of the case we should not admit any words which could possibly have an evaluative meaning; for this, in view of the way in which evaluative meaning pervades our language, would be well-nigh impossible. I only mean that we must be sure that, as we are using the words in the minor premiss, there are definite tests (not themselves involving evaluation) for ascertaining its truth or falsity. In the last paragraph I was using the word 'pleasure' in such a sense, though it is not always so used.

4. 2. The relation between the two premisses may perhaps be made clearer by considering an artificial example. Let us suppose that a man has a peculiar kind of clairvoyance such that he can know everything about the effects of all the alternative actions open to him. But let us suppose that he has so far formed for himself, or been taught, no principles of conduct. In deciding between alternative courses of action, such a man would know, fully and exactly, between what he was deciding. We have to ask to what extent, if any, such a man would be handicapped, in coming to a decision, by not having any formed principles. It would seem beyond doubt that he could choose between two courses; it would be strange, even, to call such a choice necessarily arbitrary or ungrounded; for if a man knows to the last detail exactly what he is doing, and what he might otherwise have done, his choice is not arbitrary in the sense in which a choice would be arbitrary if made by the toss of a coin without any consideration of the effects. But suppose that we were to ask such a man 'Why did you choose this set of effects rather than that? Which of the many effects were they that led you to decide the way you did?' His answer to this question might be of two kinds. He might say 'I can't give any reasons; I just felt like deciding that way; another time, faced with the same choice,

I might decide differently'. On the other hand, he might say 'It was this and this that made me decide; I was deliberately avoiding such and such effects, and seeking such and such'. If he gave the first of these two answers, we might in a certain sense of that word call his decision arbitrary (though even in that case he had *some* reason for his choice, namely, that he felt that way); but if he gave the second, we should not.

Let us see what is involved in this second type of answer. Although we have assumed that the man has no formed principles, he shows, if he gives the second answer, that he has started to form principles for himself; for to choose effects *because* they are such and such is to begin to act on a principle that such and such effects are to be chosen. We see in this example that in order to act on principle it is not necessary in some sense to have a principle already, before you act; it may be that the decision to act in a certain way, because of something about the effects of acting in that way, *is* to subscribe to a principle of action—though it is not necessarily to adopt it in any permanent sense.

Ordinary men are not so fortunate as the man in our artificial example. They start, indeed, without any knowledge of the future at all; and when they acquire knowledge it is not of this intuitive kind. The kind of knowledge that we have of the future—unless we are clairvoyant—is based upon principles of prediction which we are taught, or form for ourselves. Principles of prediction are one kind of principle of action; for to predict is to act in a certain way. Thus, although there is nothing logically to prevent someone doing entirely without principles, and making all his choices in the arbitrary manner exhibited in the first kind of answer, this never in fact occurs. Moreover, our knowledge of the future is fragmentary and only probable; and therefore in many cases the principles which we are taught or form for ourselves say, not 'Choose this kind of effect rather than that', but 'You do not know for certain what will be the effects; but do this rather than that, and the effects are most likely to be such as you would have chosen, if you had known them'. It is important to remember, in this connexion, that 'likely' and 'probable' are value-words; in many contexts 'It is probable (or likely) that P' is adequately rendered by 'There is *good* reason (or evidence) for holding that P'.

4. 3. We may distinguish, so far, two reasons why we have principles. The first reason applies to anyone, even a man with complete insight into the future, who decides to choose something because it is of a certain character. The second reason applies to us because we do not in fact have complete knowledge of the future, and because such knowledge as we do have involves principles. To these reasons a third must now be added. Without principles, most kinds of teaching are impossible, for what is taught is in most cases a principle. In particular, when we learn *to do* something, what we learn is always a principle. Even to learn or be taught a fact (like the names of the five rivers of the Punjab) is to learn how to answer a question; it is to learn the principle 'When asked "What are the names of the five rivers of the Punjab?" answer "The Jhelum, the Chenab, &c.".' By this I do not of course mean, that to learn to do anything is to learn to recite by rote some universal imperative sentence. This would involve us in a vicious regress; for learning to recite is a kind of learning, and must have its principles; but in that case we should have to learn to recite the principles of reciting. The point is rather this, that to learn to do anything is never to learn to do an individual act; it is always to learn to do acts of a certain kind in a certain kind of situation; and this is to learn a principle. Thus, in learning to drive, I learn, not to change gear *now*, but to change gear when the engine makes a certain kind of noise. If this were not so, instruction would be of no use at all; for if all an instructor could do were to tell us to change gear *now*, he would have to sit beside us for

the rest of our lives in order to tell us just when, on each
occasion, to change gear.

Thus without principles we could not learn anything whatever from our elders. This would mean that every generation
would have to start from scratch and teach itself. But even if
each generation were able to teach itself, it could not do so
without principles; for self-teaching, like all other teaching,
is the teaching of principles. This may be seen by recurring
to our artificial example. Let us suppose that our clairvoyant
made all his choices on some principle, but always forgot, as
soon as he had made the choice, what the principle had been.
He would have, accordingly, each time he made a decision,
to go over all the effects of the alternative actions. This would
be so time-consuming that he would not have the leisure to
make many decisions in the course of his life. He would spend
his whole time deciding matters like whether to step off with
the right or the left foot, and would never reach what we
should call the more important decisions. But if he could
remember the principles on which he acted, he would be in
a much better position; he could *learn* how to act in certain
kinds of circumstance; he could learn to single out quickly
the relevant aspects of a situation, including the effects of the
various possible actions, and so choose quickly, and in many
cases habitually. Thus his powers of considered decision
would be set free for more momentous decisions. When the
cabinet-maker has learnt how to make a dovetail without
thinking much about it, he will have time to think about such
things as the proportions and aesthetic appearance of the
finished product. And it is the same with our conduct in
the moral sphere; when the performance of the lesser duties
has become a matter of habit, we have time to think about
the greater.

There is a limit in practice to the amount that can be
taught to someone by someone else. Beyond this point, self-
teaching is necessary. The limit is set by the variety of

conditions which may be met with in doing whatever is being taught; and this variety is greater in some cases than in others. A sergeant can teach a recruit almost all there is to be known about fixing bayonets on parade, because one occasion of fixing bayonets on parade is much like another; but a driving instructor cannot do more than begin to teach his pupil the art of driving, because the conditions to be met with in driving are so various. In most cases, teaching cannot consist in getting the learner to perform faultlessly a fixed drill. One of the things that has to be included in any but the most elementary kinds of instruction is the opportunity for the learner to make decisions for himself, and in so doing to examine, and even modify to suit particular types of case, the principles which are being taught. The principles that are taught us initially are of a provisional kind (very like the principle 'Never say what is false' which I discussed in the last chapter). Our training, after the initial stages, consists in taking these principles, and making them less provisional; we do this by using them continually in our own decisions, and sometimes making exceptions to them; some of the exceptions are made because our instructor points out to us that certain cases are instances of classes of exceptions to the principle; and some of the exceptions we decide on for ourselves. This presents no more difficulty than our clairvoyant had in deciding between two sets of effects. If we learn from experiment that to follow a certain principle would have certain effects, whereas to modify it in a certain way would have certain other effects, we adopt whichever form of the principle leads to the effects which we choose to pursue.

We may illustrate this process of modifying principles from the example already used, that of learning to drive. I am told, for instance, always to draw into the side of the road when I stop the car; but later I am told that this does not apply when I stop before turning into a side-road to the offside—for then I must stop near the middle of the road until it is possible for me to turn. Still later I learn that in this manœuvre it is not necessary to stop at all if it is an uncontrolled junction and I can see that there is no traffic which I should obstruct by turning. When I have picked up all these modifications to the rule, and the similar modifications to all the other rules, and practice them habitually as so modified, then I am said to be a good driver, because my car is always in the right place on the road, travelling at the right speed, and so on. The good driver is, among other things, one whose actions are so exactly governed by principles which have become a habit with him, that he normally does not have to *think* just what to do. But road conditions are exceedingly various, and therefore it is unwise to let all one's driving become a matter of habit. One can never be certain that one's principles of driving are perfect—indeed, one can be very sure that they are not; and therefore the good driver not only drives well from habit, but constantly attends to his driving habits, to see whether they might not be improved; he never stops learning.[1]

It is hardly necessary to point out that principles of driving, like other principles, are normally not inculcated by their verbal repetition, but by example, demonstration, and other practical means. We learn to drive, not by precept, but by being shown how to do particular bits of driving; the precepts are usually only explanatory or mnemonic of what we are being shown. Thereafter, we try to do the particular manœuvres ourselves, and are criticized for failures, commended when we do them well, and so gradually get the hang of the various principles of good driving. For although our instruction is far from being purely verbal, nevertheless what we are being taught are principles. The fact that the derivation of particular acts (or commands to do them) from principles is normally done non-verbally does not show that it is not a logical process, any more than the inference:

[1] Cf. Romans 2[21].

> The clock has just struck seven times
> The clock strikes seven times at seven o'clock only
> ∴ It is just after seven o'clock

is shown to be non-logical because it is never made explicitly in words.

Drivers often know just what to do in a certain situation without being able to enunciate in words the principle on which they act. This is a very common state of affairs with all kinds of principles. Trappers know just where to set their traps, but often cannot explain just why they have put a trap in a particular place. We all know how to use words to convey our meaning; but if a logician presses us for the exact definition of a word we have used, or the exact rules for its use, we are often at a loss. This does not mean that the setting of traps or the use of words or the driving of cars does not proceed according to principles. One may know how, without being able to say how—though if a skill is to be taught, it is easier if we *can* say how.

We must not think that, if we can decide between one course and another without further thought (it seems self-evident to us, which we should do), this necessarily implies that we have some mysterious intuitive faculty which tells us what to do. A driver does not know when to change gear by intuition; he knows it because he has learnt and not forgotten; what he knows is a principle, though he cannot formulate the principle in words. The same is true of moral decisions which are sometimes called 'intuitive'. We have moral 'intuitions' because we have learnt how to behave, and have different ones according to how we have learnt to behave.

It would be a mistake to say that all that had to be done to a man to make him into a good driver was to tell him, or otherwise inculcate into him, a lot of general principles. This would be to leave out the factor of decision. Very soon after he begins to learn, he will be faced with situations to deal with which the provisional principles so far taught him require modification; and he will then have to decide what to do. He will very soon discover which decisions were right and which wrong, partly because his instructor tells him, and partly because having seen the effects of the decisions he determines in future not to bring about such effects. On no account must we commit the mistake of supposing that decisions and principles occupy two separate spheres and do not meet at any point. All decisions except those, if any, that are completely arbitrary are to some extent decisions of principle. We are always setting precedents for ourselves. It is not a case of the principle settling everything down to a certain point, and decision dealing with everything below that point. Rather, decision and principles interact throughout the whole field. Suppose that we have a principle to act in a certain way in certain circumstances. Suppose then that we find ourselves in circumstances which fall under the principle, but which have certain other peculiar features, not met before, which make us ask 'Is the principle really intended to cover cases like this, or is it incompletely specified—is there here a case belonging to a class which should be treated as exceptional?' Our answer to this question will be a decision, but a decision of principle, as is shown by the use of the value-word 'should'. If we decide that this should be an exception, we thereby modify the principle by laying down an exception to it.

Suppose, for example, that in learning to drive I have been taught always to signal before I slow down or stop, but have not yet been taught what to do when stopping in an emergency; if a child leaps in front of my car, I do not signal, but keep both hands on the steering-wheel; and thereafter I accept the former principle with this exception, that in cases of emergency it is better to steer than to signal. I have, even on the spur of the moment, made a decision of principle. To understand what happens in cases like this is to understand a great deal about the making of value-judgements.

4. 4. I do not wish to seem to be pressing too far my comparison, in respect of the way in which they are learnt, between principles of driving and principles of conduct. It is necessary also to bear in mind some distinctions. In the first place, the expression 'good driver' is itself ambiguous in that it is not immediately clear what standard is being applied. It might be simply a standard of expertness; we might call a person a good driver if he were able to do just what he wanted with his car; we might say 'Although a very good driver, he is most inconsiderate to other road users'. On the other hand, we sometimes expect a good driver to have moral qualities as well; we do not, according to this criterion, call a man a good driver if he drives expertly, but without the slightest heed for the convenience or safety of other people. The line between these two standards of good driving is not easy to draw in practice. There is also a third standard, according to which a driver is said to be good if he conforms to the accepted principles of good driving as laid down, for example, in the *Highway Code*. Since the *Highway Code* is compiled with a definite purpose in view, this standard coincides to a great extent with the second.

Secondly, there are two ways of looking at driving instruction:

(1) We establish at the beginning certain ends, for example the avoidance of collisions, and instruction consists in teaching what practices are conducive to those ends. According to this way of looking at them, the principles of good driving are hypothetical imperatives.

(2) We teach at first simple rules of thumb, and the learner only gradually comes to see what the ends are, at which the instruction is aimed.

It must not be thought that either (1) or (2) by itself gives a complete account of our procedure. Which method we adopt depends to a great extent on the maturity and intelligence of the learner. In teaching simple soldiers to drive, we might incline more to the second method; if I had to teach my two-year-old son to drive, I should have to adopt the same methods as I now adopt for teaching him to refrain from interfering with the controls when I am driving myself. With a highly intelligent learner, on the other hand, we may adopt a method which has more of (1) in it than of (2).

It must not be thought, however, that method (2) is ever entirely without a place even in the case of the most rational of learners. It may be that the desirability of avoiding collisions is at once understood and accepted even by comparatively stupid learners; but there are a great many more ends than this which a good driver has to aim at. He has to avoid causing many kinds of avoidable inconvenience both to himself and to others; he has to learn not to do things which result in damage to his vehicle, and so on. It is of no use to establish at the beginning a general end, 'the avoidance of avoidable inconvenience'; for 'inconvenience' is a value-word, and until he has had experience of driving, the learner will not know what sorts of situation are to count as avoidable inconvenience. The general end or principle is vacuous until by our detailed instruction we have given it content. Therefore it is always necessary to start, to some extent, by teaching our learner *what* to do, and leaving it for him to find out later *why*. We may therefore say that although moral principles, which are normally taught us when we are immature, are taught largely by method (2), and principles of driving preponderantly by method (1), there is not an absolute division between the two sorts of principle in this respect. What I have just said about first learning *what* to do, and about the initial vacuity of the general end, is borrowed from Aristotle.[1] The one fundamental distinction between principles of driving and principles of conduct is that the latter are, in Aristotle's term, 'architectonic' of the former; for the ends of

[1] *Nicomachean Ethics*, i. 4.

good driving (safety, the avoidance of inconvenience to others, the preservation of property, and so on) are justified ultimately, if justification is sought, by appeal to moral considerations.[1]

It would be folly, however, to say that there is only one way of learning a skill or any other body of principles, or of justifying a particular decision made in the practice of it. There are many ways, and I have tried to make the above account sufficiently general to cover all of them. It is sometimes said by writers on morals that we have to justify an act by reference to its effects, and that we tell which effects are to be sought, which avoided, by reference to some principle. Such a theory is that of the utilitarians, who bid us look at the effects, and examine these in the light of the principle of utility, to see which effects would maximize pleasure. Sometimes, on the other hand, it is said (as by Mr. Toulmin)[2] that an act is justified directly by reference to the principles which it observes, and these principles in their turn by reference to the effects of always observing them. Sometimes it is said that we should observe principles and ignore the effects—though for the reasons given above 'effects' cannot be here intended in the sense in which I have been using it. What is wrong with these theories is not what they say, but their assumption that they are telling us the only way to justify actions, or decide what actions to do. We do, indeed, justify and decide on actions in all these ways; for example, sometimes, if asked why we did A, we say, 'Because it was a case falling under principle P', and if asked to justify P in turn, we go into the effects of observing it and of not observing it. But sometimes, when asked the same question 'Why did you do A?' we say 'Because if I hadn't, E would have happened', and if asked what was wrong about E happening, we appeal to some principle.

The truth is that, if asked to justify as completely as pos-

---

[1] Op. cit. i. 1, 2.   [2] *Reason in Ethics*, pp. 144 ff.

sible any decision, we have to bring in both effects—to give content to the decision—and principles, and the effects in general of observing those principles, and so on, until we have satisfied our inquirer. Thus a complete justification of a decision would consist of a complete account of its effects, together with a complete account of the principles which it observed, and the effects of observing those principles—for, of course, it is the effects (what obeying them in fact consists in) which give content to the principles too. Thus, if pressed to justify a decision completely, we have to give a complete specification of the way of life of which it is a part. This complete specification it is impossible in practice to give; the nearest attempts are those given by the great religions, especially those which can point to historical persons who carried out the way of life in practice. Suppose, however, that we can give it. If the inquirer still goes on asking 'But why *should* I live like that?' then there is no further answer to give him, because we have already, *ex hypothesi*, said everything that could be included in this further answer. We can only ask him to make up his own mind which way he ought to live; for in the end everything rests upon such a decision of principle. He has to decide whether to accept that way of life or not; if he accepts it, then we can proceed to justify the decisions that are based upon it; if he does not accept it, then let him accept some other, and try to live by it. The sting is in the last clause. To describe such ultimate decisions as arbitrary, because *ex hypothesi* everything which could be used to justify them has already been included in the decision, would be like saying that a complete description of the universe was utterly unfounded, because no further fact could be called upon in corroboration of it. This is not how we use the words 'arbitrary' and 'unfounded'. Far from being arbitrary, such a decision would be the most well-founded of decisions, because it would be based upon a consideration of everything upon which it could possibly be founded.

It will be noticed how, in talking of decisions of principle, I have inevitably started talking value-language. Thus we decide that the principle *should* be modified, or that it is *better* to steer than to signal. This illustrates the very close relevance of what I have been saying in the first part of this book to the problems of the second part; for to make a value-judgement is to make a decision of principle. To ask whether I ought to do A in these circumstances is (to borrow Kantian language with a small though important modification) to ask whether or not I will that doing A in such circumstances should become a universal law.[1] It may seem a far cry from Kant to Professor Stevenson; but the same question could be put in other words by asking 'What attitude shall I adopt and recommend towards doing A in such circumstances?'; for 'attitude', if it means anything, means a principle of action. Unfortunately Stevenson, unlike Kant, devotes very little space to the examination of this first-person question; had he paid due attention to it, and avoided the dangers of the word 'persuasive', he might have reached a position not unlike that of Kant.

4. 5. As Kant points out in the important passage on the Autonomy of the Will, to which I referred earlier, we have to make our own decisions of principle.[2] Other people cannot make them for us unless we have first decided to take their advice or obey their orders. There is an interesting analogy here with the position of the scientist, who also has to rely on his own observations. It might be said that there is a difference here between decisions and observations, to the detriment of the former, in that an observation, once made, is public property, whereas decisions have to be made by the agent himself on each occasion. But the difference is only apparent. A scientist would not have become a scientist unless he had convinced himself that the observations of other

[1] Cf. *Groundwork of the Metaphysic of Morals*, tr. H. J. Paton, p. 88.
[2] Op. cit., pp. 108 ff.

scientists were in general reliable. He did this by making some observations of his own. When we learnt elementary chemistry at school, we had some theoretical periods and some practical. In the theoretical periods we studied books; in the practical periods we made experiments, and found, if we were lucky, that the results tallied with what the books said. This showed us that what the books said was not all nonsense; so that even if, by reason of disturbing factors ignored by us, our experiments came out wrong, we were inclined to trust the books and acknowledge that we had made a mistake. We were confirmed in this assumption by the fact that we often discovered later what the mistake had been. If our observations, however carefully we did them, were always at variance with the textbooks, we should not be tempted to make science our profession. Thus the confidence of the scientist in other people's observations is ultimately based, among other things, on his own observations and his own judgements about what is reliable. He has in the end to rely on himself.

The case of the moral agent is not dissimilar. When in our early days we are given our elementary moral instruction, there are some things that we are told, and some things that we do. If, when we did as we were told, the total effects of our so doing, when they happened, were always such as we would not have chosen, had we known, then we should seek better advice, or, if prevented from so doing, either work out our own salvation or become moral defectives. If we are in general given what we subsequently come to see to have been good advice, we decide in general to follow the advice and adopt the principles of those who have given us this good advice in the past. This is what happens to any child who is well brought up. Just as the scientist does not try to rewrite all that is in the textbooks, but takes that for granted and sticks to his own particular researches, so this fortunate child will take over bodily the principles of his elders and adapt them in detail, by his own decisions, to suit his own circumstances from time to time. This is how in a well-ordered society morality remains stable, and at the same time gets adapted to changing circumstances.

4. 6. There are, however, many ways in which this happy state of affairs can deteriorate. Let us consider a process that seems to occur quite often in history; it occurred in Greece during the fifth and fourth centuries, and it has occurred in our own time. Suppose that the people of a certain generation —I will call it the first generation—have got very settled principles, inherited from their fathers. Suppose that they have become so settled as to be second nature, so that generally speaking people act on the principles without thinking, and their power of making considered decisions of principle becomes atrophied. They act always by the book, and come to no harm, because the state of the world in their time remains much the same as that for which the principles were thought out. But their sons, the second generation, as they grow up, find that conditions have changed (e.g. through a protracted war or an industrial revolution), and that the principles in which they have been brought up are no longer adequate. Since, in their education, much stress has been laid on observing principles, and very little on making the decisions on which these principles are ultimately based, their morality has no roots, and becomes completely unstable. Books on 'The Whole Duty of Man' are no longer written or read. Often, when they do what it says in such books, they subsequently find cause to regret their decisions; and there are too many cases of this kind for any confidence in the old principles, as a body, to remain. No doubt there are among these old principles certain very general ones, which will remain acceptable unless human nature and the state of the world undergo a most fundamental change; but the second generation, not having been brought up to make decisions of principle, but to do what it says in the book, will not, most of them, be able to make those crucial decisions which would determine which principles to keep, which to modify, and which to abandon. Some people, the good children of the second generation, will have been so steeped in the old principles that they just follow them come what may; and these will on the whole be more fortunate than the others, for it is better to have some principles, even if they sometimes lead to decisions which we regret, than to be morally adrift. The bulk of the second generation, and still more perhaps of the third, will not know which of the principles to keep and which to reject; and so they will come more and more to live from day to day—not a bad thing, because it trains their powers of decision, but it is an unpleasant and dangerous state to be in. A few among them, the rebels, will shout from the housetops that some or all of the old moral principles are worthless; some of these rebels will advocate new principles of their own; some will have nothing to offer. Though they increase the confusion, these rebels perform the useful function of making people decide between their rival principles; and if they not only advocate new principles, but sincerely try to live by them, they are conducting a moral experiment which may be of the utmost value to man (in which case they go down in history as great moral teachers), or may, on the other hand, prove disastrous both to them and to their disciples.

It may take several generations for this disease to play itself out. Morality regains its vigour when ordinary people have learnt afresh to decide for themselves what principles to live by, and more especially what principles to teach their children. Since the world, though subject to vast material changes, changes only very slowly in matters that are fundamental from the moral point of view, the principles which win the acceptance of the mass of people are not likely to differ enormously from those which their fathers came to distrust. The moral principles of Aristotle resemble those of Aeschylus more than they differ from them, and we ourselves shall perhaps come back to something recognizably like the morality of our grandfathers. But there will be some changes; some of the principles advocated by the rebels will have been adopted. That is how morality progresses—or retrogresses. The process is, as we shall see, reflected by very subtle changes in the uses of value-words; the impossibility of translating Aristotle's catalogue of virtues into modern English may serve as an example, and the disappearance without trace of the word 'righteous' may serve as another.

4. 7. The question 'How shall I bring up my children?' which we have mentioned, is one to the logic of which, since ancient times, few philosophers have given much attention. A child's moral upbringing has an effect upon him which will remain largely untouched by anything that happens to him thereafter. If he has had a stable upbringing, whether on good principles or on bad ones, it will be extremely difficult for him to abandon those principles in later life—difficult but not impossible. They will have for him the force of an objective moral law; and his behaviour will seem to give much evidence in support of intuitionist ethical theories, provided that it is not compared with the behaviour of those who stick just as firmly to quite different principles. But nevertheless, unless our education has been so thorough as to transform us into automata, we can come to doubt or even reject these principles; that is what makes human beings, whose moral systems change, different from ants, whose 'moral system' does not. Therefore, even if for me the question 'What shall I do in such and such a situation?' is almost invariably answered without ambiguity by the moral intuition which my upbringing has given me, I may, if I ask myself 'How shall I bring up my children?' pause before giving an answer. It is here that the most fundamental moral decisions of all arise; and it is here, if only moral philosophers would pay attention to them, that the most characteristic uses of moral words are to be found. Shall I bring up my children *exactly* as I was brought up, so that they have the same intuitions about morals as I have? Or have circumstances altered, so that the moral character of the father will not provide a suitable equipment for the children? Perhaps I shall try to bring them up like their father, and shall fail; perhaps their new environment will be too strong for me, and they will come to repudiate my principles. Or I may have become so bewildered by the strange new world that, although I still act from force of habit on the principles that I have learnt, I simply do not know what principles to impart to my children, if, indeed, one in my condition can impart any settled principles at all. On all these questions, I have to make up my mind; only the most hide-bound father will try to bring up his children, without thinking, in exactly the way that he himself was brought up; and even he will usually fail disastrously.

Many of the dark places of ethics become clearer when we consider this dilemma in which parents are liable to find themselves. We have already noticed that, although principles have in the end to rest upon decisions of principle, decisions as such cannot be taught; only principles can be taught. It is the powerlessness of the parent to make for his son those many decisions of principle which the son during his future career will make, that gives moral language its characteristic shape. The only instrument which the parent possesses is moral education—the teaching of principles by example and precept, backed up by chastisement and other more up-to-date psychological methods. Shall he use these means, and to what extent? Certain generations of parents have had no doubts about this question. They have used them to the full; and the result has been to turn their children into good intuitionists, able to cling to the rails, but bad at steering round corners. At other times parents—and who shall blame them?—suffer from lack of confidence; they are not sure enough what they themselves think, to be ready to impart to their children a stable way of life. The children of such a generation are likely to grow up opportunists, well able to make individual decisions, but without the settled body of principles which is the most priceless heritage that any generation can leave to its successors. For, though principles are in the end built upon decisions of principle, the building is the work of many generations, and the man who has to start from the beginning is to be pitied; he will not be likely, unless he is a genius, to achieve many conclusions of importance, any more than the average boy, turned loose without instruction upon a desert island, or even in a laboratory, would be likely to make any of the major scientific discoveries.

The dilemma between these two extreme courses in education is plainly a false one. Why it is a false one is apparent, if we recall what was said earlier about the dynamic relation between decisions and principles. It is very like learning to drive. It would be foolish, in teaching someone to drive, to try to inculcate into him such fixed and comprehensive principles that he would never have to make an independent decision. It would be equally foolish to go to the other extreme and leave it to him to find his own way of driving. What we do, if we are sensible, is to give him a solid basis of principles, but at the same time ample opportunity of making the decisions upon which these principles are based, and by which they are modified, improved, adapted to changed circumstances, or even abandoned if they become entirely unsuited to a new environment. To teach only the principles, without giving the opportunity of subjecting them to the learner's own decisions of principle, is like teaching science exclusively from textbooks without entering a laboratory. On the other hand, to abandon one's child or one's driving-pupil to his own self-expression is like putting a boy into a laboratory and saying 'Get on with it'. The boy may enjoy himself or kill himself, but will probably not learn much science.

The moral words, of which we may take 'ought' as an example, reflect in their logical behaviour this double nature of moral instruction—as well they may, for it is in moral instruction that they are most typically used. The sentences in which they appear are normally the expression of decisions of principle—and it is easy to let the decisions get separated, in our discussion of the subject, from the principles. This is the source of the controversy between the 'objectivists', as intuitionists sometimes call themselves, and the 'subjectivists', as they often call their opponents. The former lay stress on the fixed principles that are handed down by the father, the latter on the new decisions which have to be made by the son. The objectivist says 'Of course you know what you ought to do; look at what your conscience tells you, and if in doubt go by the consciences of the vast majority of men'. He is able to say this, because our consciences are the product of the principles which our early training has indelibly planted in us, and in one society these principles do not differ much from one person to another. The subjectivist, on the other hand, says 'But surely, when it comes to the point—when I have listened to what other people say, and given due weight to my own intuitions, the legacy of my upbringing—I have in the end to decide for myself what I ought to do. To deny this is to be a conventionalist; for both common moral notions and my own intuitions are the legacy of tradition, and—apart from the fact that there are so many different traditions in the world—traditions cannot be started without someone doing what I now feel called upon to do, decide. If I refuse to make my own decisions, I am, in merely copying my fathers, showing myself a lesser man than they; for whereas they must have initiated, I shall be merely accepting.' This plea of the subjectivist is quite justified. It is the plea of the adolescent who wants to be adult. To become morally adult is to reconcile these two apparently conflicting positions by learning to make decisions of principle; it is to learn to use 'ought'-sentences in the realization that they can only be verified by reference to a standard or set of principles which we have by our own decision accepted and made our own. This is what our present generation is so painfully trying to do.

PART II

'GOOD'

'Good. . . . The most general adjective of commendation, implying the existence in a high, or
at least satisfactory, degree of characteristic
qualities which are either admirable in themselves, or useful for some purpose . . .'
Oxford English Dictionary

5

'NATURALISM'

5. 1. THE first part of this book has served two purposes.
First, by examining in some detail the language used for
expressing commands—the simplest form of prescription—
we are now in a better position to understand the more complex logical behaviour of value-words, the other main instrument for prescribing with which our language provides us.
Secondly, we have, in the course of this examination, had
occasion to look at some of the kinds of situation in which we
are accustomed to use prescriptive language, and seen how
we do learn to answer questions of the form 'What shall I
do?', to which the answer is a prescription.

In the remainder of the book I shall be dealing with some
typical value-words, and especially with 'good', 'right', and
'ought'. Although my selection is conventional, three explanations require to be made here. First, I do not wish to imply
that the characteristics of value-words to which I shall draw
attention are confined to the few typical words that are here
examined; it is in fact the case—and this has been productive
of logical confusion—that almost every word in our language
is capable of being used on occasion as a value-word (that
is, for commending or its opposite); and usually it is only by

cross-examining a speaker that we can tell whether he is so using a word. The word 'brilliant' is a good example. In confining attention to the simplest, most typical and most general value-words, my only object is simplicity of exposition. Secondly, the terms 'value-words' and 'evaluative' are exceedingly hard to define. I shall for the time being content myself with giving examples and illustrations; it is not until later (11. 2) that I shall be able to hazard a definition, and even then without much confidence. Thirdly, I shall follow a procedure similar to that used earlier in connexion with the learning of principles; I shall illustrate the peculiarities of value-words by examples drawn from their non-moral uses, and only later ask whether these same peculiarities are to be found in moral contexts. This procedure, though it may seem perverse, has one great advantage; it will enable me, I hope, to show that the peculiarities of these words have nothing to do with morals as such, and that therefore theories which purport to explain them have to be applicable, not only to expressions like 'good man', but also to expressions like 'good chronometer'; and to realize this is to be preserved from a number of errors.

5. 2. Let me illustrate one of the most characteristic features of value-words in terms of a particular example. It is a feature sometimes described by saying that 'good' and other such words are the names of 'supervenient' or 'consequential' properties. Suppose that a picture is hanging upon the wall and we are discussing whether it is a good picture; that is to say, we are debating whether to assent to, or dissent from, the judgement 'P is a good picture'. It must be understood that the context makes it clear that we mean by 'good picture' not 'good likeness' but 'good work of art'—though both these uses would be value-expressions.

First let us notice a very important peculiarity of the word 'good' as used in this sentence. Suppose that there is another picture next to P in the gallery (I will call it Q). Suppose that either P is a replica of Q or Q of P, and we do not know which, but do know that both were painted by the same artist at about the same time. Now there is one thing that we cannot say; we cannot say 'P is exactly like Q in all respects save this one, that P is a good picture and Q not'. If we were to say this, we should invite the comment, 'But how can one be good and the other not, if they are exactly alike? There must be some *further* difference between them to make one good and the other not.' Unless we at least admit the relevance of the question 'What makes one good and the other not?' we are bound to puzzle our hearers; they will think that something has gone wrong with our use of the word 'good'. Sometimes we cannot specify just what it is that makes one good and the other not; but there always must be something. Suppose that in the attempt to explain our meaning we said: 'I didn't say that there *was* any other difference between them; there is just this one difference, that one is good and the other not. Surely you would understand me if I said that one was *signed* and the other not, but that there was otherwise no difference? So why shouldn't I say that one was *good* and the other not, but that there was otherwise no difference?' The answer to this protest is that the word 'good' is not like the word 'signed'; there is a difference in their logic.

5. 3. The following reason might be suggested for this logical peculiarity: there is some one characteristic or group of characteristics of the two pictures on which the characteristic 'good' is logically dependent, so that, of course, one cannot be good and the other not, unless these characteristics vary too. To quote a parallel case, one picture could not be *rectangular* and the other not, unless certain other characteristics also varied, for example the size of at least one of the angles. And so a natural response to the discovery that 'good' behaves as it does, is to suspect that there is a set of characteristics which together *entail* a thing being good, and to set out to discover what these characteristics are. This is the genesis of that group of ethical theories which Professor Moore called 'naturalist'—an unfortunate term, for as Moore says himself, substantially the same fallacy may be committed by choosing metaphysical or suprasensible characteristics for this purpose.[1] Talking about the supernatural is no prophylactic against 'naturalism'. The term has, unfortunately, since Moore's introduction of it, been used very loosely. It is best to confine it to those theories against which Moore's refutation (or a recognizable version of it) is valid. In this sense most 'emotive' theories are not naturalist, though they are often called so. Their error is a quite different one. I shall argue below (11. 3) that what is wrong with naturalist theories is that they leave out the prescriptive or commendatory element in value-judgements, by seeking to make them derivable from statements of fact. If I am right in this opinion, my own theory, which preserves this element, is not naturalist.

We have to inquire, then, whether there is any characteristic or group of characteristics which is related to the characteristic of being good in the same way as the angle-measurements of figures are related to their rectangularity. In what way are the latter related? This involves answering the question: Why cannot it be the case that one picture is rectangular and the other not .unless the angle-measurements of the two pictures also differ? The answer is clearly that 'rectangular' *means* 'rectilinear and having all its angles of a certain size, namely, 90 degrees'; and, therefore, that when we have said that one picture is rectangular and the other not, we have said that the measurements of their angles differ; and if we then go on to say that they do not differ, we contradict ourselves. Therefore, to say 'P is exactly like Q in all respects save this one, that P is a rectangular picture and Q not', may be self-contradictory; whether it is self-contradictory depends on what we intend to include in 'all respects'.

[1] *Principia Ethica*, p. 39.

If we intend to include the measurements of the angles, then the sentence is self-contradictory; for it is self-contradictory to say 'P is exactly like Q in all respects, *including the measurements of its angles*, save this one, that P is a rectangular picture and Q not'; this contains the assertion that the angles of P both differ and do not differ from those of Q.

Thus the impossibility that we are speaking of is a logical one, which depends upon the meaning of the word 'rectangular'. This is a very elementary example of a logical impossibility; there are other more complex examples. Those who in recent times have denied that there can be synthetic *a priori* truth have been asserting that all *a priori* impossibility can be shown to be of this character, i.e. dependent on the meanings assigned to the words used. Whether they are right is still a matter under dispute; but for the purposes of my argument I shall assume that they are. The dispute has reached the stage when it cannot be argued on abstract grounds alone, but only by the painstaking analysis of particular sentences which are claimed to be true *a priori* and yet synthetic.[1]

5. 4. Let us then ask whether 'good' behaves in the way that we have noticed for the same reason that 'rectangular' does; in other words, whether there are certain characteristics of pictures which are defining characteristics of a good picture, in the same way as 'having all its angles 90 degrees and being a rectilinear plane figure' are defining characteristics of a rectangle. Moore thought that he could prove that there were no such defining characteristics for the word 'good' as used in morals. His argument has been assailed since he propounded it; and it is certainly true that the formulation of it was at fault. But it seems to me that Moore's argument was not merely plausible; it rests, albeit insecurely, upon a secure foundation; there is indeed something about the way in which, and the purposes for which, we use the word 'good'

---

[1] An excellent example of such analysis is to be found in an article on 'The Incongruity of Counterparts', by D. F. Pears, *Mind*, lxi (1952), 78.

which makes it impossible to hold the sort of position which Moore was attacking, although Moore did not see clearly what this something was. Let us, therefore, try to restate Moore's argument in a way which makes it clear why 'naturalism' is untenable, not only for the moral use of 'good' as he thought, but also for many other uses.

Let us suppose for the sake of argument that there are some 'defining characteristics' of a good picture. It does not matter of what sort they are; they can be a single characteristic, or a conjunction of characteristics, or a disjunction of alternative characteristics. Let us call the group of these characteristics C. 'P is a good picture' will then mean the same as 'P is a picture and P is C'. For example, let C mean 'Having a tendency to arouse in people who are at that time members of the Royal Academy (or any other definitely specified group of people), a definitely recognizable feeling called "admiration"'. The words 'definitely specified' and 'definitely recognizable' have to be inserted, for otherwise we might find that words in the *definiens* were being used evaluatively, and this would make the definition no longer 'naturalistic'. Now suppose that we wish to say that the members of the Royal Academy have good taste in pictures. To have good taste in pictures means to have this definitely recognizable feeling of admiration for those pictures, and only those pictures, which are good pictures. If therefore we wish to say that the members of the Royal Academy have good taste in pictures, we have, according to the definition, to say something which means the same as saying that they have this feeling of admiration for pictures which have a tendency to arouse in them this feeling.

Now this is not what we wanted to say. We wanted to say that they admired good pictures; we have succeeded only in saying that they admired pictures which they admired. Thus if we accept the definition we debar ourselves from saying something that we do sometimes want to say. What this something is will become apparent later; for the moment let us say that what we wanted to do was to *commend* the pictures which the members of the Royal Academy admired. Something about our definition prevented our doing this. We could no longer commend the pictures which they admired, we could only say that they admired those pictures which they admired. Thus our definition has prevented us, in one crucial case, from commending something which we want to commend. That is what is wrong with it.

Let us generalize. If 'P is a good picture' is held to mean the same as 'P is a picture and P is C', then it will become impossible to commend pictures for being C; it will be possible only to say that they are C. It is important to realize that this difficulty has nothing to do with the particular example that I have chosen. It is not because we have chosen the wrong defining characteristics; it is because, whatever defining characteristics we choose, this objection arises, that we can no longer commend an object for possessing those characteristics.

Let us illustrate this by another example. I am deliberately excluding for the moment moral examples because I want it to be clear that the logical difficulties which we are encountering have nothing to do with morals in particular, but are due to the general characteristics of value-words. Let us consider the sentence 'S is a good strawberry'. We might naturally suppose that this means nothing more than 'S is a strawberry and S is sweet, juicy, firm, red, and large'. But it then becomes impossible for us to say certain things which in our ordinary talk we do say. We sometimes want to say that a strawberry is a good strawberry because it is sweet, &c. This—as we can at once see if we think of ourselves saying it—does not mean the same as saying that a strawberry is a sweet, &c., strawberry because it is sweet, &c. But according to the proposed definition this is what it would mean. Thus here again the proposed definition would prevent our saying something that we do succeed in saying meaningfully in our ordinary talk.

5. 5. It has sometimes been alleged against Moore's refutation of naturalism that it proves too much—that if it were valid for 'good' it would be valid for any word whatever that is claimed to be definable in terms of other words. Certain phrases of Moore's lay him open to this objection, especially his quotation of Butler's slogan 'Everything is what it is, and not another thing'.[1] Of course, what the naturalists are claiming is that 'goodness' is not 'another thing' than the characteristics which they claim to be its defining characteristics. If naturalism were true and were consistently held, the naturalist could argue as follows: 'When I say that x is a good A and when I say that it is an A which is C, I am saying one and the same thing, just as when I say that y is a puppy and when I say that y is a young dog I am saying one and the same thing. A refutation on your lines could be produced of the theory that "puppy" means "young dog". It would proceed as follows: If you accept this definition, then the sentence "A puppy is a young dog" becomes equivalent to "A young dog is a young dog", and this is something that we would never want to say; but we do sometimes say "A puppy is a young dog"; therefore the proposed definition prevents our saying something that in our ordinary talk we do meaningfully say, &c.'

In order to answer this objection, let us inquire on what occasions and for what purpose we use the sentence 'A puppy is a young dog'. It is, I think, clear that we should normally use this sentence as a definition; we should use it when we were explaining what a puppy was or what the word 'puppy' meant. It is not a sentence that would normally be used to say anything of substance about puppies, though I shall consider in a moment one such possible use. Thus this

[1] For an excellent criticism of this side of Moore's refutation, see A. N. Prior, *Logic and the Basis of Ethics*, ch. i.

sentence has little difference in meaning, if any, from the original definition ' "Puppy" means "young dog" '. This does not imply that either form of the definition has anything wrong with it *as a definition*. A definition, if it is a correct one, is always analytic in one sense and synthetic in another. Taken as a sentence about puppies it is analytic; taken as a sentence about the word 'puppy' it is synthetic. It is never a synthetic sentence about puppies; if it were it would not be a definition but something else.

This may be made clear by a consideration of our example. The sentence 'A puppy is a young dog', although it is normally used as a definition of the word 'puppy', is none the less misleading in its form; for it has the same form as some sentences which are not definitions—e.g. 'A puppy is a queer thing to find inside a beer-barrel'. It is misleading because it is elliptical, and this obscures the fact that it is a definition. We could correct both these faults at the cost of a certain artificiality by saying instead 'The English sentence "If anything is a puppy it is a young dog (and vice versa)" is analytic'. This has the merit of disentangling the synthetic from the analytic elements of the original definition. The part within inverted commas is analytic if the definition is correct; for the function of the definition is to say that it is analytic. On the other hand, the whole sentence is not analytic; it is a synthetic assertion about the part within inverted commas; we find out whether the assertion is correct or not by studying English usage. Thus the whole sentence is a synthetic assertion about words; the part within inverted commas has the form of an assertion about puppies, but asserts nothing about them because it is analytic. Nowhere in the whole sentence is there a synthetic assertion about puppies.

5. 6. There is one conceivable case in which 'A puppy is a young dog' might be used to make a synthetic assertion about puppies. It might be parallel to 'A tadpole is a young frog (or other batrachian)', which might be used to inform a person that the class of animals which he had learnt to distinguish by the name 'tadpole' did in fact turn into frogs when they grew up. But this case cannot be used in support of the objection. Suppose that it were objected 'You cannot refute naturalism in the way that you seek to; for in this case you would have to abandon also the definition of "tadpole" as "young frog"; it could be argued that the sentence "A tadpole is a young frog", which we all agree can be used to make a synthetic assertion about tadpoles (namely that they grow into frogs), is, according to this definition, a mere tautology'. It is not difficult to see that this objection rests upon an equivocation. We cannot at the same time maintain that 'tadpole' means the same as 'young frog' and that 'A tadpole is a young frog' is a synthetic assertion. Either we have to define 'tadpole' independently of 'young frog' (for example by ostensive definition, by pointing at a lot of tadpoles swimming in the pond), in which case 'A tadpole is a young frog' will indeed be a synthetic assertion, but 'tadpole' will mean not 'young frog' but 'the sort of animal you can see swimming in the pond there'; or else we have to define 'tadpole' as 'young frog', in which case 'A tadpole is a young frog' becomes analytic and 'Those are tadpoles swimming in the pond there' becomes, not an ostensive definition, but a statement of fact to the effect that those animals swimming in the water will turn into frogs when they grow up. In fact, of course, we learn the meaning of 'tadpole' in both these ways, and it is to that extent equivocal. This does not worry us, because cases do not arise in which animals just like these turn, not into frogs, but into, say, snakes; but if we did find a species of snake that had young just like a tadpole, we should have to make the distinction, by saying 'Before you can tell whether an animal like this is really a tadpole, you have to wait and see whether it turns into a frog or a snake'; or we might adopt other expedients. This is a familiar puzzle in logic; we shall have occasion to recur to it later (7. 5; 11. 2).

It is possible to argue that there is a similar 'equivocation' about the word 'good'; for, as we shall see, it has both descriptive and evaluative force, and these have to be learnt by different means and independently of one another. But we are not yet in a position to explain this.

Here it will suffice to point out that if it is interpreted in this way the objection misses the point. For my argument is that we cannot say that 'x is a good A' means the same as 'x is an A which is C', because then it becomes impossible to commend A's which are C by saying 'A's which are C are good A's'. In the 'tadpole' case the parallel argument would be 'You cannot say that "x is a tadpole" means the same as "x is a young frog", because then it becomes impossible to say that tadpoles turn into frogs by saying "A tadpole is a young frog".' But, of course, if we do stick to the definition of 'tadpole' as equivalent to 'young frog', then it is indeed impossible to say this; it is only because 'tadpole' is sometimes used otherwise than according to this definition, that we are able sometimes to use 'A tadpole is a young frog' as a synthetic assertion. And similarly, it is because 'good' is sometimes (indeed in almost all cases) used otherwise than according to 'naturalistic' definitions, that we can use it in order to commend.

5. 7. But let us return to the sentence 'A puppy is a young dog', and, neglecting the possible synthetic use which we have been considering, confine our attention to its use as a definition of 'puppy'. The objection which we are considering maintains that we do sometimes meaningfully say 'A puppy is a young dog', and that by this we do not mean the same as we would if we said 'A young dog is a young dog'. Let us therefore expand both these sentences in the way previously suggested. They become, respectively, 'The English sentence "If anything is a puppy it is a young dog" is analytic' and 'The English sentence "If anything is a young dog it is a young dog" is analytic'. Both these sentences are true, but they do not mean the same; and it is interesting to notice that here is one case in which, although 'puppy' means the same as 'young dog', they cannot be substituted for one another without change of meaning. But this is not in the least paradoxical. It is well known that, if a sentence contains another sentence within it in inverted commas, it is not always possible without changing the meaning of the whole sentence to substitute synonymous expressions for expressions inside the inverted commas. Thus the sentence 'He said "It is a puppy"' does not mean the same as the sentence 'He said "It is a young dog"'; for his actual words are being reported, and it makes a difference what they were. Similarly, the sentence 'It says in the dictionary "Puppy: young dog"' is not the same in meaning as the sentence 'It says in the dictionary "Young dog: young dog"'. Similarly, again, the sentence 'When Englishmen say "puppy" they mean the same as "young dog"' does not have the same meaning as the sentence 'When Englishmen say "young dog" they mean the same as "young dog"'. And so, also, 'The English sentence "If anything is a puppy it is a young dog" is analytic' does not mean the same as 'The English sentence "If anything is a young dog it is a young dog" is analytic'. And therefore the abbreviations of these sentences, 'A puppy is a young dog' and 'A young dog is a young dog' do not mean the same.

But all this is entirely irrelevant to the case of the word 'good'. The force of the objection was, that our attack upon naturalistic definitions of the word 'good' could be pressed equally against definitions of the word 'puppy', and that, since these latter are obviously in order, there must be something wrong with the attack. Now our attack upon naturalistic definitions of 'good' was based upon the fact that if it were true that 'a good A' meant the same as 'an A which is C', then it would be impossible to use the sentence 'An A which is C is good' in order to commend A's which are C; for this sentence would be analytic and equivalent to 'An A which is

C is C'. Now it seems clear that we do use sentences of the form 'An A which is C is good' in order to commend A's which are C; and that when we do so, we are not doing the same sort of thing as when we say 'A puppy is a young dog'; that is to say, commending is not the same sort of linguistic activity as defining. The meaning of expressions like 'A puppy is a young dog' is preserved by expanding them into overt definitions like 'The English sentence "If anything is a puppy it is a young dog" is analytic'. This latter sentence is true, and is verifiable by consulting the usage of educated Englishmen. Which Englishmen are to count as educated is, of course, a value-question about proper word-usage, but that is not here relevant. On the other hand, a sentence of the form 'An A which is C is good' cannot without change of meaning be rewritten 'The English sentence "An A which is C is good" is analytic'. For a sentence of the latter type certainly could not be used for commending, whereas sentences of the former type can be and are; we commend strawberries which are sweet, &c., by saying 'A strawberry which is sweet, &c., is good', but we never do this by saying 'The English sentence "A strawberry which is sweet, &c., is good" is analytic'. This latter sentence, if it were used, would not be a commendation of sweet strawberries; it would be a remark—and a false one—about the English language.

5. 8. Thus it is not true to say that the means used to upset naturalistic definitions of value-terms could be used equally to upset any definition. Value-terms have a special function in language, that of commending; and so they plainly cannot be defined in terms of other words which themselves do not perform this function; for if this is done, we are deprived of a means of performing the function. But with words like 'puppy' this does not apply; one may define 'puppy' in terms of any other words which will do the same job. Whether two expressions will do the same job is decided by reference to usage. And since what we are trying to do is to give an account of the word 'good' as it *is* used—not as it *might* be used if its meaning and usage were changed—this reference is final. It is therefore no answer to the above argument to claim that a 'naturalist' might if he pleased define 'good' in terms of some characteristics of his choice. Such an arbitrary definition is quite out of place here; the logician is, it is true, at liberty to define his own technical terms as he pleases, provided that he makes it clear how he is going to use them. But 'good' in this context is not a technical term used for talking about what the logician is talking about; it itself *is* what he is talking about; it is the object of his study, not the instrument. He is studying the function of the word 'good' in language; and so long as he wishes to study this, he must continue to allow the word the function which it has in language, that of commending. If by an arbitrary definition he gives the word a different function from that which it now has, then he is not studying the same thing any longer; he is studying a figment of his own devising.

Naturalism in ethics, like attempts to square the circle and to 'justify induction', will constantly recur so long as there are people who have not understood the fallacy involved. It may therefore be useful to give a simple procedure for exposing any new variety of it that may be offered. Let us suppose that someone claims that he can deduce a moral or other evaluative judgement from a set of purely factual or descriptive premisses, relying on some definition to the effect that V (a value-word) means the same as C (a conjunction of descriptive predicates). We first have to ask him to be sure that C contains no expression that is covertly evaluative (for example 'natural' or 'normal' or 'satisfying' or 'fundamental human needs'). Nearly all so-called 'naturalistic definitions' will break down under this test—for to be genuinely naturalistic a definition must contain no expression for whose applicability there is not a definite criterion which does not involve the making of a value-judgement. If the definition satisfies this test, we have next to ask whether its advocate ever wishes to commend anything for being C. If he says that he does, we have only to point out to him that his definition makes this impossible, for the reasons given. And clearly he cannot say that he never wishes to commend anything for being C; for to commend things for being C is the whole object of his theory.

6

MEANING AND CRITERIA

6. 1. The argument of the preceding chapter establishes that 'good', being a word used for commending, is not to be defined in terms of a set of characteristics whose names are not used for commending. This does not mean that there is *no* relation between what have been called 'good-making' characteristics and 'good'; it means only that this relation is not one of entailment. What the relation is, I shall discuss later. But before that it is necessary to guard against a mistake into which it was easy to fall, when it had been shown that 'good' was not analysable in the way that naturalism suggests. This was the mistake of supposing that, because 'good' was not the name of a complex property ('good strawberry', for example, meaning 'strawberry that is sweet, juicy, firm, red, and large'), it must therefore be the name of a simple property. Of course, if all that is meant by 'property' is 'whatever an adjective stands for', then it is harmless to say that 'good' is the name of a simple property, except in so far as it suggests that there is for every adjective something to which it stands in this superficially simple, but philosophically baffling relation. But because 'property' is not normally used in such a broad sense as this, the use of the word in this connexion has led to serious confusion; it has led to comparisons between 'good' and typical simple property-words like 'red'. It is this comparison that must now be examined. Since it is, in fact, very difficult to establish a logical criterion for distinguishing simple from complex properties, I shall not confine the argument as narrowly as this comparison would suggest; the arguments which I shall use tell equally against the theory that 'good' is the name of a complex property, in the commonly accepted sense. They are complementary to another series of arguments marshalled with great skill by Mr. Toulmin against a similar theory.[1]

It is characteristic of the word 'red' that we can explain its meaning in a certain way. The suggestion that the logical character of words can be investigated by asking how we would explain their meaning comes from Wittgenstein. The point of the method is that it brings out the ways in which the learner could get the meaning *wrong*, and so helps to show what is required in order to get it right. Let us suppose that we are trying to teach English to a foreign philosopher who either deliberately or inadvertently makes all the mistakes that he *logically* can (for what mistakes anyone *actually* makes or avoids is irrelevant). We must assume that, when we start, he knows no English, and we know nothing of his language. At a certain stage, we shall get to the simple property-words. If we had to explain the meaning of the word 'red' to such a person, we might proceed as follows: we might take him to see pillar-boxes, tomatoes, underground trains, &c., and say, as we showed him each object, 'That is red'. And then we might take him to see some pairs of things that were like each other in most respects, but unlike in colour (for example pillar-boxes in England and Ireland, ripe and unripe tomatoes, London Transport trains and main line electric trains), and on each occasion say 'This is red; that is not red but green'. In this way he would learn the use of the word 'red'; he would become conversant with its meaning.

It is tempting to assume that the meaning of all words that are applied in any sense to things could be conveyed (directly or indirectly) in the same way; but this is not so, as is well known. The word 'this' could not be treated in this fashion, nor, perhaps, could the word 'Quaxo'—if we can call the name of a cat a word at all. It is instructive to ask whether the meaning of 'good' could be explained like this, and if not, why not.

6. 2. It is a characteristic of 'good' that it can be applied

---

[1] *Reason in Ethics*, ch. ii.

to any number of different classes of objects. We have good cricket-bats, good chronometers, good fire-extinguishers, good pictures, good sunsets, good men. The same is true of the word 'red'; all the objects I have just listed might be red. We have to ask first, whether, in explaining the meaning of the word 'good', it would be possible to explain its meaning in all of these expressions at once, or whether it would be necessary to explain 'good cricket-bat' first, and then go on to explain 'good chronometer' in the second lesson, 'good fire-extinguisher' in the third, and so on; and if the latter, whether in each lesson we should be teaching something entirely new—like teaching the meaning of 'fast dye' after we had in a previous lesson taught the meaning of 'fast motor-car'—or whether it would be just the same lesson over again, with a different example—like teaching 'red dye' after we had taught 'red motor-car'. Or there might be some third possibility.

The view that 'good chronometer' would be a completely new lesson, even though the day before we had taught 'good cricket-bat', runs at once into difficulties. For it would mean that at any one time our learner could only use the word 'good' in speaking of classes of objects which he had learnt so far. He would never be able to go straight up to a new class of objects and use the word 'good' of one of them. When he had learnt 'good cricket-bat' and 'good chronometer', he would not be able to manage 'good fire-extinguisher'; and when he had learnt the latter, he would still be unable to manage 'good motor-car'. But in fact one of the most noticeable things about the way we use 'good' is that we are able to use it for entirely new classes of objects that we have never called 'good' before. Suppose that someone starts collecting cacti for the first time and puts one on his mantel-piece— the only cactus in the country. Suppose then that a friend sees it, and says 'I must have one of those'; so he sends for one from wherever they grow, and puts it on his mantel-piece, and when his friend comes in, he says 'I've got a better cactus than yours'. But how does he know how to apply the word in this way? He has never learnt to apply 'good' to cacti; he does not even know any *criteria* for telling a good cactus from a bad one (for as yet there are none); but he has learnt to use the word 'good', and having learnt that, he can apply it to any class of objects that he requires to place in order of merit. He and his friend may dispute about the criteria of good cacti; they may attempt to set up rival criteria; but they could not even do this unless they were from the start under no difficulty in using the word 'good'. Since, therefore, it is possible to use the word 'good' for a new class of objects without further instruction, learning the use of the word for one class of objects cannot be a different lesson from learning it for another class of objects—though learning the criteria of goodness in a new class of objects may be a new lesson each time.

It is strange that the use of 'good cacti' should not be a new lesson; for good cacti seem to have little in common with good chronometers, and good chronometers with good cricket-bats. Yet somehow we seem to be able to learn the use of the word without being taught *what* in a particular class of objects entitles us to apply it to a member of that class. Suppose that, in teaching the meaning of 'good', we determine not to be put off by the apparent dissimilarities of good chronometers, cacti, and cricket-bats; suppose that we go on trying at all costs to find something that we can point to in any class of objects whatever, and say 'There you are, that's what makes a thing good; when you've learnt to identify that elusive quality, you will know the meaning of the word'. This seems at first sight a natural procedure; for if the use of the word 'good' is common to all classes of objects, it must have a common meaning; and it is natural to suppose that if it has a common meaning, there is a common property to which it refers, like 'red'.

Such efforts are doomed to failure. But even if we fail to

find a common property for *all* classes of objects, members of which are called good, we may try to carry out the programme in a less ambitious way; we may give up the struggle to find one common property, and content ourselves with dividing the uses of the word into a few groups, within each of which the word refers to a common property. Thus we may think that in the first lesson we may be able to teach the meaning of the word in its 'intrinsic' use, and then in the second lesson go on to teach the 'instrumental' use, and so on.

This procedure also runs into difficulties. People who have suggested it have usually been most interested in 'intrinsic' good; and therefore they have divided off 'instrumental' good only in order to ignore it. This has meant that they have also ignored the immense difficulties of dealing with 'instrumental' good in this fashion. I propose to adopt the opposite programme; I shall put 'intrinsic' good on one side for the moment, and ask whether it is possible to treat 'instrumental' goodness as a common ostensible property.

6. 3. There are two different possible variants of the suggested procedure. One seeks to explain the meaning of 'good', as used 'instrumentally', on the assumption that the common property which we are looking for is that of being conducive to good in the 'intrinsic' sense. This will hardly do; for we call many things 'good so-and-sos' in an instrumental way which are not conducive to 'intrinsic' good; for example, good pistols (which are as good pistols in the hands of the murderer as in those of the police); here, granted the assumption that there is one 'instrumental' use of the word, it seems that the word 'good' is being used in just the same way as in 'good chronometer'. Good chronometers, too, are not always conducive to intrinsic good—not if they are used for navigating aircraft which are going to drop atom bombs on the chosen people (whichever that is).

The other variant seeks to explain the meaning of the word 'good' as used 'instrumentally' on the assumption that it means the same as 'efficient', that is to say, 'conducive to the end that it is used for'. Now it is possible that 'good' does sometimes mean this; I am not at the moment discussing whether it does or not, but whether, if it does, 'being conducive to the end that it is used for' is the sort of property that we could teach our foreigner to identify in one lesson. Let us suppose that we try. We take him round to a lot of people who are doing things with things, and say to him 'That is a good X', 'That is not a good Y', and so on. But suppose that he is, or pretends to be, rather obtuse. We take him to see cricket-bats and chronometers and fire-extinguishers, and point out, in each case, which are good and which are not. But he still refuses to admit that he can recognize a property common to good members of all these three classes. His difficulty is obvious. Good fire-extinguishers differ from bad fire-extinguishers in putting out flames quickly, without fumes, &c.; good chronometers differ from bad ones in giving Greenwich time, being easily readable, &c.; good cricket-bats differ from bad ones in hitting balls far and fast, not stinging, &c.; but there seems to be little in common to all these three performances that he can learn to recognize. We call them all 'the ends for which the objects are used'; but this common designation presents the same difficulty as we were having with the word 'good' itself. For unless we can teach him, in the case of any new class of objects, to recognize without assistance for what end they are being used, we shall still have to go on giving him a new lesson each time, though it will be not about the word 'good' but about the word 'end'. And the fact that the word 'end' presents the same problems as the word 'good' suggests that the problems have the same source in both cases. We remember that Aristotle, who made the word 'end' a technical term in philosophy, defined it as 'a good to be achieved by action'.[1]

6. 4. There is a certain class of words which we may call,

[1] *Nicomachean Ethics*, 1097^{a}23, 1141^{b}12.

in a wide sense, 'functional words'. A word is a functional word if, in order to explain its meaning fully, we have to say what the object it refers to is *for*, or what it is supposed to do. Functional words include, not only the names of instruments in the narrow sense, but also the names of technicians and techniques. We do not know what a carpenter is until we know what a carpenter is supposed to do. Similarly with an auger; we do not know what an auger is, until we know, in the words of the *Shorter Oxford English Dictionary*, not only that it has 'a long pointed shank, &c.', but also that it is 'a carpenter's tool for boring holes in wood, &c.' We could not explain the meaning of 'auger' to our foreigner in this sense by showing him a lot of augers, and teaching him to recognize an auger when he saw one. He might be able to do this infallibly, and still not know what augers are for, and so not know fully the meaning of the word as the dictionary gives it.

It is more conducive to clarity to regard the peculiarities of sentences like 'this is not a good auger', which we shall be considering, as due to this feature of the word 'auger' (the fact that it is a functional word) than to say that the word 'good' has a special meaning in this sentence. In this sentence we are handed on a plate, in virtue of the meanings of the words used, one of the necessary criteria of a good auger; but we are handed it by the word 'auger', not by the word 'good'. We saw above that it is possible to construct 'hypothetical' imperative sentences which are derivable from indicative minor premisses alone, and that this is done by including the required imperative major premiss as part of the conclusion, inside an 'if'-clause. We have here a somewhat similar operation. To know what an auger is for is to know the end that augers are supposed to fulfil; it is to know that being able to bore holes is a necessary condition of being a good auger, or that if any auger will not bore holes it is not a good auger. But if we define 'auger' in such a way that this major premiss is analytic, then by including the word 'auger' in the conclusion 'This is not a good auger' we make this conclusion derivable from the indicative minor premiss alone, 'This auger will not bore holes'.

But to know what an auger is for, is to have no more than a very rudimentary knowledge of the criteria of a good auger; it is to know one necessary condition only. Holes may be bored with very bad augers. We can indeed say that if an auger will not bore holes at all, then it is certainly a bad one; but this is as far as the definition of 'auger' by itself takes us. For this reason, 'good auger' means a lot more than 'auger which is conducive to the end that augers are used for, *sc.* boring holes'; it means at least 'auger which is conducive to fulfilling *well* the end that augers are used for, *sc.* to boring holes *well*'. And so even if our foreigner knew what an auger was, there would be a lot that we should have to teach him still about the criteria of a good auger. We should have to teach him, for example, that a good auger does not blister the hands, is not rusty, and bores holes that have clean edges.

Let us ask, however, what would be involved in teaching our foreigner this minimum, that an auger is for boring holes. We should have to take him to see people boring holes with augers. He would have to know what they were trying to do. If he thought that they were just trying to exercise their wrists, we should not be able by this demonstration to explain to him what an auger is for. Now to try to produce a result is to *choose*, subject to the limitations of our knowledge and power, to do those things which are conducive to that result. Thus to try to make a hole is to choose to do those things (including selecting those instruments) which are conducive to a hole's being made.

This same word 'choose' obtrudes itself if we seek to explain, not what an auger is used for, but what it is designed for. To design an instrument for boring holes is to choose to have it made in such a way that it is conducive to boring holes. The fact that the word 'choose' obtrudes itself in this way is of great interest. To choose is to answer a question of the form 'What shall I do?' The man who is designing an instrument for boring holes asks himself 'Of what design shall I have this instrument made?' and answers 'Of such a design that it will be conducive to boring holes'; the man who is trying to bore holes asks himself 'What sort of instrument shall I employ?' and answers 'The sort of instrument that will be conducive to boring holes'. Thus we have here an important tie-up between the present discussion and that of the first part of this book. But let us return to our foreigner. It is by now established that *if* we can explain to him what choosing is—or if he knows already—then we shall be able to explain how to find out, in the case of any instrument, what it is for; and that if we can explain this, we can also give him some rudimentary explanation of how to tell a good member of any class of instruments from a bad one. If, on the other hand, he does not understand what choosing is, he will not understand any of our explanations.

It is therefore apparent, that we have here a similar situation to that which we noticed earlier. To teach *what makes* a member of any class a good member of the class is indeed a new lesson for each class of objects; but nevertheless the word 'good' has a constant meaning which, once learnt, can be understood no matter what class of objects is being discussed. We have, as I have already said, to make a distinction between the meaning of the word 'good' and the criteria for its application. Even in the case of instrumental goodness, there is not one common criterion for all classes of objects. We still have to teach our learner something new each time. It is true that the words 'conducive to' will occur in all our explanations; but there will occur after these words some other expression, such as 'boring holes' or 'keeping exact time' which will be different in each case. If instead of all these different expressions we write the common expression '. . . what the instrument is for', we reintroduce an expression whose meaning is not explicable by the 'red' technique. It requires an understanding of what it is to choose; and this understanding is necessary, whether we make the reference to it in explaining the meaning of 'auger' or 'chronometer', or whether we explain the meanings of these words (inadequately) simply by showing examples, and leave the reference to choosing until we have to explain 'good auger' or 'good chronometer'.

Thus the notion of 'instrumental good', which was introduced in order to mitigate the difficulty of 'a new lesson for each class of objects', fails in this purpose. To sum up: there is no common property which is recognizable in all cases where a member of a class—no matter what class—is said to be 'instrumentally good'. Even if, therefore, we divide the uses of the word 'good' into certain broad classes, 'instrumental good', 'intrinsic good', and so on, we still cannot apply the technique of explanation within those classes that we apply with the word 'red'. We can teach the criteria for applying the word 'good' within a particular class; but this does not teach the meaning of the word. A man could even learn to tell good augers from bad, without in the least knowing what 'good' meant; he could, that is to say, learn to sort out augers into piles, good and bad, and do this quite correctly, but still not realize that this classification was for the purpose of selecting some augers *in preference* to others. Suppose, for example, that he was coming with us on a long voyage of exploration, and we said to him 'Don't forget to bring an auger', and he brought one of the bad ones; we should think that he did not know the meaning of 'good auger', although quite able to tell a good auger from a bad one.

6. 5. I will now describe a way in which, provided that our foreigner knew the meaning of the word 'choose', I might indeed be able to explain the meaning of 'good' to him in one lesson, the paradoxical character of which will emphasize the point that I have been making. Suppose that I ask him to teach me one of the games of his own country, and he says that he will teach me about the game of *smashmak*. This game, he explains, is played with a thing called a *shmakum*. Before asking him to describe to me a shmakum, or to proceed with his account of the game, I say to him 'Where do you get these shmakums from?' and he answers 'From shmakum-makers; in our country every town has a street of shmakum-makers'. I then ask 'Suppose you are buying a new shmakum, and you go to this street, and all sorts of shmakums are offered you, all about the same price, what sort of shmakum would you choose?'; and he replies 'All other things being equal, I would choose the one that I could make the most *smashes* with'. I then make a bold venture, and say 'Ah! I see, then you think the *best* shmakum is the one that you could make most smashes with'.

Now it might well puzzle my learner that I can say this. We must assume that he has learnt, on the analogy with other adjectives, that 'best' is the superlative of 'good'. But the strange thing is that, although I do not know how the game of smashmak is played, or what a shmakum is like, or what it is to make smashes, I have, on the strength simply of his telling me that he would *choose*, all other things being equal, the shmakum with which he could make the most smashes, ventured to suggest that he thinks that this sort of shmakum is the best sort of shmakum. How, he may well ask, can I tell what properties he thinks shmakums, with which he could make the most smashes, have, except that he could make the most smashes with them—I who know nothing about the game?

Now we must examine this opinion which I have attributed to him, to see some of its logical characteristics. The opinion is:

The best shmakum is the one that I could make the most smashes with.

Let us call this sentence, A. And let us notice, first of all, that

A does not mean the same as the following sentence, which I will call B:

The expression 'the best shmakum' means 'the shmakum that I could make the most smashes with'.

For if I said that he thought B, I should be attributing to him an opinion which, in his circumstances, it would be very odd for him to hold; for it is an opinion about the equivalence in meaning of a word ('best') and a phrase ('that I could make the most smashes with'); and since he does not know (nor even think he knows) the meaning of the word 'best', how can he have opinions about what phrases are equivalent to it?

Let us detail the position again; *I* know the meaning of the word 'best', but do not know the meanings of 'shmakum' or 'smash'; *he* knows the meanings of the latter expressions, but not of 'best'. And so neither of us is really in a position to say B. But I have said that he thinks A; that is to say, I have attributed to him an opinion, not about the meaning of words, but about what, as a matter of substance, is the best shmakum—an opinion which, if either of us had the necessary knowledge of the meanings of the words to be used, could be put into words by saying A.

Moreover, I have now got, by this manœuvre, into the position of being able to explain to him, in one lesson, the meaning of 'best', and therefore of 'good'. For I have caught him, as it were, *having the thought* about shmakums for which the appropriate linguistic expression is A. It is a thought which has something to do with choosing or being inclined to choose. The paradoxical feature of this explanation is, that it is conducted with reference to a class of objects (shmakums) the criteria for the goodness of which I do not know. This shows that to explain the meaning of 'good' is quite different from explaining any of the various criteria for its application. The explanation is not, of course, a logical analysis, for we are not concerned in this chapter with logical analyses; but it is at least a sketch of the sort of way in which a person who did not know the meaning of 'good' might be helped to pick it up.

6. 6. At this point a superficial observer might misinterpret the procedure which I have used in explaining the meaning of the word 'good'. For it might be said, 'Surely it can now be seen that the word "good" is like the word "red" after all. It refers to a common property, only this common property has the characteristic of being, unlike redness, inaccessible in a peculiar way. It is in fact the property of producing or being in some way associated with certain inner experiences, which cannot be experienced except by the person who is having them; these experiences may be called purposive or preferential, and instances of them are what we refer to as "trying", "aiming at", "preferring", "choosing", &c. Of course', the objection goes on, 'if a word refers to a certain sort of experience, you cannot define it ostensively to someone who has never had that experience; but this is equally true of "red". You cannot define "red" ostensively to someone who has never had the experience of seeing a red object.' The effect of this objection would be to undo all my argument; for I have been maintaining that 'good' is unlike 'red' in that its meaning is independent of the criteria for its application; but if the criterion for the application of 'good' is the having of certain purposive or preferential experiences, it is no longer possible to distinguish meaning from criteria in the way that I have been trying to do. For it might be that it was possible to explain the meaning of 'good' to my foreigner by getting him to have these experiences and then telling him that the word 'good' was properly applied to the objects of them; and this would make 'good' just like 'red'—for you explain the meaning of 'red' also by getting the learner to have certain experiences and telling him that the word 'red' is properly applied to the objects of them. I require, therefore, to destroy the hypothesis that the meaning of the word 'good' is fully explained by saying that it is properly applied to the objects of certain recognizable experiences. It is worth while noticing here that this is a familiar theory in relation to 'good' in moral contexts; for it is sometimes said that in these contexts we tell whether or not to apply the word 'good' to an object solely by observing whether or not we have certain experiences towards that object—experiences, for example, of 'moral approval' or of a 'sense of fittingness'.

We must notice that at the crucial point in the last stage of my explanation of the word 'good' to my foreigner, what happened was this: I learnt from him that all other things being equal he would choose a shmakum with which he could make the most smashes; and on the strength of this, I told him that he *thought* that the best shmakum was the one with which he could make the most smashes. I did not tell him on the strength of it that the best shmakum *was* the one with which he could make the most smashes; and this point is of fundamental importance. For, while it may be the case that if I know that X would choose, all other things being equal, the shmakum with which he could, &c., I am more or less safe in saying 'X *thinks* that the best shmakum is the one with which he could, &c.', it is by no means the case that I am safe in saying 'the best shmakum *is* the one with which X could, &c.' For suppose that my learner misconstrued my remark and thought that he could correctly apply the word 'best' to any member of a class which he, as a matter of fact, would choose, all other things being equal. Then suppose that I ask him to tell me which is the best of a number of hockey-sticks; he may choose the one with which he, as a beginner in the game, could miss the ball least often, and say 'This is the best one; I know this is right after what you have told me about the word "best"; for this is the one that I would choose'. But then I have to explain to him that he has made a mistake; for that he would choose that hockey-stick shows, not that it is the best, but that he thinks that it is the best.

What the learner has done can be made clear as follows. He has gone on, in spite of adverse experiences, assuming that criteria and meaning are the same. Therefore, having quite correctly learnt, from my previous remark, that the thought that he had when he chose or was inclined to choose a certain sort of shmakum was correctly expressed by saying that the best shmakum was, &c., and that having learnt this, he had learnt the *meaning* of the word 'good', not only as applied to shmakums, but as applied to anything else, he naturally thought that he had also learnt something about the *criteria* for applying the word. But in fact he had learnt nothing at all about the criteria for applying the word. For about the criteria for shmakums he knew already, and about the criteria for other things he was no whit the wiser, since they are all different from the criteria for shmakums. What he had learnt was the *meaning* of the word, and nothing about its *criteria*. And since criteria are different from meaning, it would be perfectly possible for him to use the word in the full knowledge of its meaning, but, through ignorance of the right criteria, apply it to the wrong objects. Thus, even if he had not misconstrued my remark in the manner described in the last paragraph, and even if he had correctly learnt the meaning of 'good', he might still say 'The best hockey-stick is the one with which I can miss the ball least often'; and in so doing, he might be using the word 'good' correctly to express the thought that he had about hockey-sticks—namely, his choosing or being inclined to choose such a hockey-stick; but he would, of course, be choosing a sort of hockey-stick which we, who know the criteria for choosing hockey-sticks, know to be a bad sort of hockey-stick to choose.

It is, moreover, not necessary to believe in 'inner experiences' in order to commit the confusion to which I have just referred. The same mistake could be made by one

who interpreted the word 'choose' entirely in terms of 'preferential behaviour'. The fact that a person, or set of people,
behave preferentially towards a certain member of a class is
not in itself a necessary or sufficient condition for saying that
it is a good member of the class; it is only the most important
of the many things that might make us want to say that they
think that it is a good member. Suppose that we are investigating the meaning of 'good drink'. We find that Americans
behave preferentially towards coca-cola, and Russians towards vodka, and that they apply to these drinks, respectively,
the word 'good' and its Russian counterpart. But this is no
indication of a distinction in meaning between the English
and the Russian word. It merely shows what sorts of drink
Americans and Russians think good; it is a help towards
discovering the criteria of good drink current in America and
Russia respectively. Needless to say, this confusion is not
confined to the question of good drink—all those who think
that they can find out what 'good' means by studying preferential behaviour are destined to discover the following
infallible guide to conduct: that they should go on doing just
as they are doing, or as most of the people whom they
study do.[1]

It must be explained that I have ignored so far one common sense of the word 'mean' in which it is obviously untrue
to say that meaning is different from criteria. Suppose that
I had finally succeeded in teaching my foreigner what 'good'
meant in the sense of that word that I have been using so far,
and to celebrate the achievement we went for a tour to his
country and turned out to watch a game of smashmak. Then
suppose that he said to me 'That fellow just going out on to
the field is the best smashmak player in our country'; I might
ask 'How do you mean, the best player?' and he might reply
'I mean he always scores the largest number of smashes'. Here

[1] See, for further discussion of this point, my review in *Mind*, lx (1951),
430, of *Value, a Co-operative Enquiry*, ed. Ray Lepley.

it is obvious that what I was asking for, and was given, were the criteria for calling him the best player; I might equally well have said 'What makes you call him the best player?' And it is also obvious that I could not ask 'How do you mean, the best player?' (in this second sense of 'mean' in which it has to do with criteria), unless I already knew what the expression 'the best player' *meant* (in the first sense of 'mean' in which it has nothing to do with criteria). I do not wish in the least to deny the existence of this meaning of the word 'mean' in such contexts; it has indeed, through being confused with the other sense of the word on which I have been concentrating, been responsible for most of the trouble that I have been trying to clear up.

7

DESCRIPTION AND EVALUATION

7. 1. Of all the problems raised by the preceding argument, the key problem is as follows: there are two sorts of things that we can say, for example, about strawberries; the first sort is usually called *descriptive*, the second sort *evaluative*. Examples of the first sort of remark are, 'This strawberry is sweet' and 'This strawberry is large, red, and juicy'. Examples of the second sort of remark are 'This is a good strawberry' and 'This strawberry is just as strawberries ought to be'. The first sort of remark is often given as a reason for making the second sort of remark; but the first sort does not by itself entail the second sort, nor vice versa. Yet there seems to be some close logical connexion between them. Our problem is: 'What is this connexion?'; for no light is shed by saying that there is a connexion, unless we can say what it is.

The problem may also be put in this way: if we knew all the descriptive properties which a particular strawberry had (knew, of every descriptive sentence relating to the strawberry, whether it was true or false), and if we knew also the meaning of the word 'good', then what else should we require to know, in order to be able to tell whether a strawberry was a good one? Once the question is put in this way, the answer should be apparent. We should require to know, what are the criteria in virtue of which a strawberry is to be called a good one, or what are the characteristics that make a strawberry a good one, or what is the standard of goodness in strawberries. We should require to be given the major premiss. We have already seen that we can know the meaning of 'good strawberry' without knowing any of these latter things—though there is also a sense of the sentence 'What does it mean to call a strawberry a good one?' in which we should not know the answer to it, unless we also knew the answer to these other questions. It is now time to elucidate and distinguish these two ways in which we can be said to know what it means to call an object a good member of its class. This will help us to see more clearly both the differences and the similarities between 'good' and words like 'red' and 'sweet'.

Since we have been dwelling for some time on the differences, it will do no harm now to mention some of the similarities. For this purpose, let us consider the two sentences 'M is a red motor-car' and 'M is a good motor-car'. It will be noticed that 'motor-car', unlike 'strawberry', is a functional word, as defined in the preceding chapter. Reference to the *Shorter Oxford English Dictionary* shows that a motor-car is a carriage, and a carriage a means of conveyance. Thus, if a motor-car will not convey anything, we know from the definition of motor-car that it is not a good one. But when we know this, we know so little, compared with what is required in order to know the full criteria of a good motor-car, that I propose in what follows to ignore, for the sake of simplicity, this complicating factor. I shall treat 'motor-car' as if it did not have to be defined functionally: that is to say, I shall assume that we could learn the meaning of 'motor-car' (as in a sense we can) simply by being shown examples of motor-cars. It is, of course, not always easy to say whether or not a word is a functional word; it depends, like all questions of meaning, on how the word is taken by a particular speaker.

The first similarity between 'M is a red motor-car' and 'M is a good motor-car' is that both can be, and often are, used for conveying information of a purely factual or descriptive character. If I say to someone 'M is a good motor-car', and he himself has not seen, and knows nothing of M, but does on the other hand know what sorts of motor-car we are accustomed to call 'good' (knows what is the accepted standard of goodness in motor-cars), he undoubtedly receives information from my remark about what sort of motor-car it is. He will complain that I have misled him, if he subsequently discovers that M will not go over 30 m.p.h., or uses as much oil as petrol, or is covered with rust, or has large holes in the roof. His reason for complaining will be the same as it would have been if I had said that the car was red and he subsequently discovered that it was black. I should have led him to expect the motor-car to be of a certain description when in fact it was of a quite different description.

The second similarity between the two sentences is this. Sometimes we use them, not for actually conveying information, but for putting our hearer into a position subsequently to use the word 'good' or 'red' for giving or getting information. Suppose, for example, that he is utterly unfamiliar with motor-cars in the same sort of way as most of us are unfamiliar with horses nowadays, and knows no more about motor-cars than is necessary in order to distinguish a motor-car from a hansom cab. In that case, my saying to him 'M is a good motor-car' will not give him any information about M, beyond the information that it is a motor-car. But if he is able then or subsequently to examine M, he will have learnt something. He will have learnt that some of the characteristics which M has are characteristics which make people—or at any rate me—call it a good motor-car. This may not be to learn very much. But suppose that I make judgements of this sort about a great many motor-cars, calling some good and some not good, and he is able to examine all or most of the motor-cars about which I am speaking; he will in the end learn quite a lot, always presuming that I observe a consistent standard in calling them good or not good. He will eventually, if he pays careful attention, get into the position in which he knows, after I have said that a motor-car is a good one, what sort of a motor-car he may expect it to be—for example fast, stable on the road, and so on.

Now if we were dealing, not with 'good', but with 'red', we should call this process 'explaining the meaning of the word'—and we might indeed, in a sense, say that what I have been doing is explaining what one means by 'a good motor-car'. This is a sense of 'mean' about which, as we have seen, we must be on our guard. The processes, however, are very similar. I might explain the meaning of 'red' by continually saying of various motor-cars 'M is a red motor-car', 'N is not a red motor car', and so on. If he were attentive enough, he would soon get into a position in which he was able to use the word 'red' for giving or getting information, at any rate about motor-cars. And so, both with 'good' and with 'red', there is this process, which in the case of 'red' we may call 'explaining the meaning', but in the case of 'good' may only call it so loosely and in a secondary sense; to be clear we must call it something like 'explaining or conveying or setting forth the standard of goodness in motor-cars'.

The standard of goodness, like the meaning of 'red', is normally something which is public and commonly accepted. When I explain to someone the meaning of 'red motor-car', he expects, unless I am known to be very eccentric, that he will find other people using it in the same way. And similarly, at any rate with objects like motor-cars where there is a commonly accepted standard, he will expect, having learnt from me what is the standard of goodness in motor-cars, to be able, by using the expression 'good motor-car', to give information to other people, and get it from them, without confusion.

A third respect in which 'good motor-car' resembles 'red motor-car' is the following: both 'good' and 'red' can vary as regards the exactitude or vagueness of the information which they do or can convey. We normally use the expression 'red motor-car' very loosely. Any motor-car that lies somewhere between the unmistakably purple and the unmistakably orange could without abuse of language be called a red motor-car. And similarly, the standard for calling motor-cars

good is commonly very loose. There are certain characteristics, such as inability to exceed 30 m.p.h., which to anyone
but an eccentric would be sufficient conditions for refusing
to call it a good motor-car; but there is no precise set of
accepted criteria such that we can say 'If a motor-car satisfies
these conditions, it is a good one; if not, not'. And in both
cases we could be precise if we wanted to. We could, for certain purposes, agree not to say that a motor-car was 'really
red' unless the redness of its paint reached a certain measur-
able degree of purity and saturation; and similarly, we might
adopt a very exact standard of goodness in motor-cars. We
might refuse the name 'good motor-car' to any car that would
not go round a certain race-track without mishap in a certain
limited time, that did not conform to certain other rigid
specifications as regards accommodation, &c. This sort of
thing has not been done for the expression 'good motor-car';
but, as Mr. Urmson has pointed out, it has been done by the
Ministry of Agriculture for the expression 'super apple'.[1]

It is important to notice that the exactness or looseness of
their criteria does absolutely nothing to distinguish words
like 'good' from words like 'red'. Words in both classes may
be descriptively loose or exact, according to how rigidly the
criteria have been laid down by custom or convention. It certainly is not true that value-words are distinguished from
descriptive words in that the former are looser, descriptively,
than the latter. There are loose and rigid examples of both
sorts of word. Words like 'red' can be extremely loose, without becoming to the least degree evaluative; and expressions
like 'good sewage effluent' can be the subject of very rigid
criteria, without in the least ceasing to be evaluative.

It is important to notice also, how easy it is, in view of these
resemblances between 'good' and 'red', to think that there are
no differences—to think that to set forth the standard of
goodness in motor-cars is to set forth the meaning, in all

[1] *Mind*, lix (1950), 152 (also in *Logic and Language*, ii, ed. Flew, 166).

senses that there are of that word, of the expression 'good motor-car'; to think that 'M is a good motor-car' means neither more nor less than 'M has certain characteristics of which "good" is the name'.

7. 2. It is worth noticing here that the functions of the word 'good' which are concerned with information could be performed equally well if 'good' had no commendatory function at all. This can be made clear by substituting another word, made up for the purpose, which is to be supposed to lack the commendatory force of 'good'. Let us use 'doog' as this new word. 'Doog', like 'good', can be used for conveying information only if the criteria for its application are known; but this makes it, unlike 'good', altogether meaningless until these criteria are made known. I make the criteria known by pointing out various motor-cars, and saying 'M is a doog motor-car', 'N is not a doog motor-car', and so on. We must imagine that, although 'doog' has no commendatory force, the criteria for doogness in motor-cars which I am employing are the same as those which, in the previous example, I employed for goodness in motor-cars. And so, as in the previous example, the learner, if he is sufficiently attentive, becomes able to use the word 'doog' for giving or getting information; when I say to him 'Z is a doog motor-car', he knows what characteristics to expect it to have; and if he wants to convey to someone else that a motor-car Y has those same characteristics, he can do so by saying 'Y is a doog motor-car'.

Thus the word 'doog' does (though only in connexion with motor-cars) half the jobs that the word 'good' does—namely, all those jobs that are concerned with the giving, or learning to give or get, information. It does not do those jobs which are concerned with commendation. Thus we might say that 'doog' functions just like a descriptive word. First my learner learns to use it by my giving him examples of its application, and then he uses it by applying it to fresh examples. It would be quite natural to say that what I was doing was teaching my learner the *meaning* of 'doog'; and this shows us again how natural it is to say that, when we are learning a similar lesson for the expression 'good motor-car' (i.e. learning the criteria of its application), we are learning its meaning. But with the word 'good' it is misleading to say this; for the meaning of 'good motor-car' (in another sense of 'meaning') is something that might be known by someone who did not know the criteria of its application; he would know, if some-one said that a motor-car was a good one, that he was com-mending it; and to know that, would be to know the meaning of the expression. Further, as we saw earlier (6. 4), someone might know about 'good' all the things which my learner learnt about the word 'doog' (namely, how to apply the word to the right objects, and use it for giving and getting informa-tion) and yet be said not to know its meaning; for he might not know that to call a motor-car good was to commend it.

7. 3. It may be objected by some readers that to call the descriptive or informative job of 'good' its *meaning* in any sense is illegitimate. Such objectors might hold that the meaning of 'good' is adequately characterized by saying that it is used for commending, and that any information we get from its use is not a question of meaning at all. When I say 'M is a good motor-car', my meaning, on this view, is to commend M; if a hearer gets from my remark, together with his knowledge of the standard habitually used by me in assessing the merits of motor-cars, information about what description of motor-car it is, this is not part of my meaning; all my hearer has done is to make an inductive inference from 'Hare has usually in the past commended motor-cars of a certain description' and 'Hare has commended M' to 'M is of the same description'. I suspect that this objection is largely a verbal one, and I have no wish to take sides against it. On the one hand, we must insist that to know the criteria for applying the word 'good' to motor-cars is not to know—at any rate in the full or primary sense—the meaning of the expression 'good motor-car'; to this extent the objection must be agreed with. On the other hand, the relation of the expression 'good motor-car' to the criteria for its application is very like the relation of a descriptive expression to its defining characteristics, and this likeness finds an echo in our language when we ask 'What do you mean, good?', and get the answer 'I mean it'll do 80 and never breaks down'. In view of this undoubted fact of usage, I deem it best to adopt the term 'descriptive meaning'. Moreover, it is natural to say that a sentence has descriptive meaning, if the speaker intends it primarily to convey information; and when a newspaper says that X opened the batting on a good wicket, its intention is not primarily to commend the wicket, but to inform its readers what description of wicket it was.

7. 4. It is time now to justify my calling the descriptive meaning of 'good' secondary to the evaluative meaning. My reasons for doing so are two. First, the evaluative meaning is constant for every class of object for which the word is used. When we call a motor-car or a chronometer or a cricket-bat or a picture good, we are commending all of them. But because we are commending all of them for different reasons, the descriptive meaning is different in all cases. We have knowledge of the evaluative meaning of 'good' from our earliest years; but we are constantly learning to use it in new descriptive meanings, as the classes of objects whose virtues we learn to distinguish grow more numerous. Sometimes we learn to use 'good' in a new descriptive meaning through being taught it by an expert in a particular field—for example, a horseman might teach me how to recognize a good hunter. Sometimes, on the other hand, we make up a new descriptive meaning for ourselves. This happens when we start having a standard for a class of objects, certain members of which we have started needing to place in order of merit, but for which there has hitherto been no standard, as in the 'cactus' example (6. 2). I shall in the next chapter discuss why we commend things.

The second reason for calling the evaluative meaning primary is, that we can use the evaluative force of the word in order to *change* the descriptive meaning for any class of objects. This is what the moral reformer often does in morals; but the same process occurs outside morals. It may happen that motor-cars will in the near future change considerably in design (e.g. by our seeking economy at the expense of size). It may be that then we shall cease giving the name 'a good motor-car' to a car that now would rightly and with the concurrence of all be allowed that name. How, linguistically speaking, would this have happened? At present, we are roughly agreed (though only roughly) on the necessary and sufficient criteria for calling a motor-car a good one. If what I have described takes place, we may begin to say 'No cars of the nineteen-fifties were really good; there weren't any good ones till 1960'. Now here we cannot be using 'good' with the same descriptive meaning as it is now generally used with; for some of the cars of 1950 do indubitably have those characteristics which entitle them to the name 'good motor-car' in the 1950 descriptive sense of that word. What is happening is that the evaluative meaning of the word is being used in order to shift the descriptive meaning; we are doing what would be called, if 'good' were a purely descriptive word, redefining it. But we cannot call it that, for the evaluative meaning remains constant; we are rather altering the standard. This is similar to the process called by Professor Stevenson 'persuasive definition';[1] the process is not necessarily, however, highly coloured with emotion.

We may notice here that there are two chief ways in which a change in standard may be reflected in, and indeed partly effected by, a change in language. The first is the one which I have just illustrated; the evaluative meaning of 'good' is retained, and is used in order to alter the descriptive meaning and so establish a new standard. The second does not often

[1] *Ethics and Language*, ch. ix.

occur with the word 'good'; for that word is so well-established
as a value-word that the procedure would be practically impossible. This procedure is for the word to be gradually
emptied of its evaluative meaning through being used more
and more in what I shall call a conventional or 'inverted-
commas' way; when it has lost all its evaluative meaning it
comes to be used as a purely descriptive word for designating
certain characteristics of the object, and, when it is required
to commend or condemn objects in this class, some quite
different value-word is imported for the purpose. The two
processes may be illustrated and contrasted by a somewhat
over-schematized account of what has happened in the last
two centuries to the expression 'eligible bachelor'. 'Eligible'
started off as a value-word, meaning 'such as should be
chosen (*sc.* as a husband for one's daughters)'. Then, because
the criteria of eligibility came to be fairly rigid, it acquired a
descriptive meaning too; a person, if said to be eligible, might,
in the eighteenth century, have been expected to have
large landed estates and perhaps a title. By the nineteenth
century, however, the criteria of eligibility have changed;
what makes a bachelor eligible is no longer necessarily landed
property or a title; it is substantial wealth of any kind provided that it is well-secured. We might imagine a nineteenth-
century mother saying 'I know he is not of noble birth; but
he's eligible all the same, because he has £3,000 a year in the
Funds, and much more besides when his father dies'. This
would be an example of the first method. On the other hand,
in the twentieth century, partly as a reaction from the over-
rigid standards of the nineteenth, which resulted in the word
'eligible' lapsing into a conventional use, the second method
has been adopted. If now someone said 'He is an eligible
bachelor', we could almost feel the inverted commas round
the word, and even the irony; we should feel that if that was
all that could be said for him, there must be something wrong
with him. For commending bachelors, on the other hand, we

now use quite different words; we say 'He is likely to make a very *good* husband for Jane', or 'She was very *sensible* to say "yes"'.

The close connexion of standards of values with language is illustrated by the plight of the truly bilingual. A writer equally at home in English and French relates that once, when walking in the park on a rainy day, he met a lady dressed in a way which the English would call sensible, but the French *ridicule*; his mental reaction to this had to be expressed bilingually, because the standards he was applying were of diverse origin; he found himself saying to himself (slipping from English into French) 'Pretty adequate armour. How uncomfortable though. Why go for a walk if you feel like this? *Elle est parfaitement ridicule.*' This cleavage of standards is said sometimes to produce neuroses in bilinguals, as might be expected in view of the close bearing of standards of values upon action.[1]

7. 5. Although with 'good' the evaluative meaning is primary, there are other words in which the evaluative meaning is secondary to the descriptive. Such words are 'tidy' and 'industrious'. Both are normally used to commend; but we can say, without any hint of irony, 'too tidy' or 'too industrious'. It is the descriptive meaning of these words that is most firmly attached to them; and therefore, although we must for certain purposes class them as value-words (for if we treat them as purely descriptive, logical errors result), they are so in a less full sense than 'good'. If the evaluative meaning of a word, which was primary, comes to be secondary, that is a sign that the standard to which the word appeals has become conventional. It is, of course, impossible to say *exactly* when this has happened; it is a process like the coming of winter.

Although the evaluative meaning of 'good' is primary, the

[1] P. H. J. Lagarde-Quost, 'The Bilingual Citizen', *Britain Today*, Dec. 1947, p. 13; Jan. 1948, p. 13.

secondary descriptive meaning is never wholly absent. Even
when we are using the word 'good' evaluatively in order to
set up a new standard, the word still has a descriptive meaning, not in the sense that it is used to *convey* information, but
in the sense that its use in setting up the new standard is an
essential preliminary—like definition in the case of a purely
descriptive word—to its subsequent use with a new descriptive meaning. It is also to be noticed that the relative promin-
ence of the descriptive and evaluative meanings of 'good'
varies according to the class of objects within which commendation is being given. We may illustrate this by taking
two extreme examples. If I talk of 'a good egg', it is at once
known to what description of egg I am referring—namely, one
that is not decomposed. Here the descriptive meaning pre-
dominates, because we have very fixed standards for assessing
the goodness of eggs. On the other hand, if I say that a poem
is a good one, very little information is given about what
description of poem it is—for there is no accepted standard
of goodness in poems. But it must not be thought that 'good
egg' is exclusively descriptive, or 'good poem' exclusively
evaluative. If, as the Chinese are alleged to do, we chose to
eat eggs that are decomposed, we should call that kind of egg
good, just as, because we choose to eat game that is slightly
decomposed, we call it 'well-hung' (compare also the expression 'good Stilton cheese'). And if I said that a poem was
good, and was not a very eccentric person, my hearer would
be justified in assuming that the poem was not 'Happy birth-
day to you!'

In general, the more fixed and accepted the standard, the
more information is conveyed. But it must not be thought
that the evaluative force of the word varies at all exactly in
inverse proportion to the descriptive. The two vary independently: where a standard is firmly established and is as
firmly believed in, a judgement containing 'good' may be
highly informative, without being any the less commen-

datory. Consider the following description of the Oxford Sewage Farm:

> The method employed is primitive but efficient. The farm is unsightly, obnoxious to people dwelling near it, and not very remunerative, but the effluent from it is, in the technical sense, good.[1]

Now here, as may be seen by consulting handbooks on the subject, there are perfectly well-recognized tests for determining whether effluent is good or bad. One manual[2] gives a simple field test, and another[3] gives a series of more comprehensive tests which take up seventeen pages. This might tempt us to say that the word is used in a purely descriptive sense and has no evaluative force. But, although admittedly in calling effluent good in this technical sense we are commending it as effluent and not as perfume, we are nevertheless commending it; it is not a neutral chemical or biological fact about it that it is good; to say that it was bad would be to give a very good reason for sacking the sewage-farmer or taking other steps to see that it was good in future. The proper comment on such a lapse was made by a former Archbishop of York, speaking to the Congress of the Royal Sanitary Institute, 1912:

> There is now, I hope, no need of the trenchant eloquence of that noble-hearted pioneer of sanitary science, Charles Kingsley, to insist that it is not religion, but something more nearly approaching blasphemy, to say that an outbreak of disease is God's will being done, when patently it is man's duty which is being left undone.[4]

It is true that, if the word 'good' in a certain sentence has very little evaluative meaning, it is likely that it has a fair

[1] *Social Services in the Oxford District, vol.* 1, p. 322.
[2] Kershaw, *Sewage Purification and Disposal,* pp. 213–14.
[3] Thresh, Beale, and Suckling, *The Examination of Waters and Water Supplies,* 6th ed., ch. xx.
[4] Kershaw, op. cit., p. 4.

amount of descriptive meaning, and vice versa. That is because, if it had very little of either, it would have very little meaning at all, and would not be worth uttering. To this extent the meanings vary inversely. But this is only a tendency; we may do justice to the logical phenomena by saying that 'good' normally has at least some of both sorts of meaning; that it normally has sufficient of both sorts taken together to make it worth uttering; and that, provided that the first two conditions are satisfied, the amounts of the two sorts of meaning vary independently.

There are, however, cases in which we use the word 'good' with no commendatory meaning at all. We must distinguish several kinds of such non-commendatory uses. The first has been called the *inverted-commas* use. If I were not accustomed to commend any but the most modern styles of architecture, I might still say 'The new chamber of the House of Commons is very good Gothic revival'. I might mean this in several senses. The first is that in which it is equivalent to 'a good example to choose, if one is seeking to illustrate the typical features of Gothic revival' or 'a good specimen of Gothic revival'. This is a specialized evaluative sense, with which we are not here concerned. I might mean, on the other hand, 'genuinely preferable to most other examples of Gothic revival, and therefore to be commended *within* the class of Gothic revival buildings, though not within the class of buildings in general'. With this sense, too, we are not now concerned; it is a commendatory use, with a limited class of comparison (8. 2). The sense with which we are concerned is that in which it means, roughly, 'the sort of Gothic revival building about which a certain sort of people—you know who —would say "that is a good building".' It is characteristic of this use of 'good' that in expanding it we often want to put the word 'good' inside inverted commas; hence the name. We are, in this use, not making a value-judgement ourselves, but alluding to the value-judgements of other people. This type of use is extremely important for the logic of moral judgements, in which it has caused some confusion.

It is to be noticed that it is easiest to use 'good' in an inverted-commas sense when a certain class of people, who are sufficiently numerous and prominent for their value-judgements to be well known (e.g. the 'best' people in any field), have a rigid standard of commendation for that class of object. In such cases, the inverted-commas use can verge into an *ironic* use, in which not only is no commendation being given, but rather the reverse. If I had a low opinion of Carlo Dolci, I might say 'If you want to see a really "good" Carlo Dolci, go and look at the one in . . .'.

There is another use in which the absence of evaluative content is not sufficiently obvious to the speaker for us to call it either an inverted-commas or an ironic use. This is the *conventional* use, in which the speaker is merely paying lip-service to a convention, by commending, or saying commendatory things about, an object just because everyone else does. I might, if I myself had no preference at all about the design of furniture, still say 'This piece of furniture is of good design', not because I wished to guide my own or anyone else's choice of furniture, but simply because I had been taught the characteristics which are generally held to be criteria of good design, and wished to show that I had 'good taste' in furniture. It would be difficult in such a case to say whether I was evaluating the furniture or not. If I were not a logician, I should not ask myself the questions which would determine whether I was. Such a question would be 'If someone (not connected in any way with the furniture trade), consistently and regardless of cost filled his house with furniture not conforming to the canons by which you judge the design of this furniture to be good, would you regard that as evidence that he did not agree with you?' If I replied 'No, I would not; for what furniture is of good design is one question, and what furniture one chooses for oneself is another', then we might conclude that I had not been really commending the design by calling it good, but only paying lip-service to a convention. We shall recur to this sort of cross-examination later (11. 2).

These are only some of the many ways in which we use the word 'good'. A logician cannot do justice to the infinite subtlety of language; all he can do is to point out some of the main features of our use of a word, and thereby put people on their guard against the main dangers. A full understanding of the logic of value-terms can only be achieved by continual and sensitive attention to the way we use them.

8

COMMENDING AND CHOOSING

8. 1. IT is now time to inquire into the reasons for the logical features of 'good' that we have been describing, and to ask why it is that it has this peculiar combination of evaluative and descriptive meaning. The reason will be found in the purposes for which it, like other value-words, is used in our discourse. The examination of these purposes will reveal the relevance of the matters discussed in the first part of this book to the study of evaluative language.

I have said that the primary function of the word 'good' is to commend. We have, therefore, to inquire what commending is. When we commend or condemn anything, it is always in order, at least indirectly, to guide choices, our own or other people's, now or in the future. Suppose that I say 'The South Bank Exhibition is very good'. In what context should I appropriately say this, and what would be my purpose in so doing? It would be natural for me to say it to someone who was wondering whether to go to London to see the Exhibition, or, if he was in London, whether to pay it a visit. It would, however, be too much to say that the reference to choices is always as direct as this. An American returning from London to New York, and speaking to some people who had no intention of going to London in the near future, might still make the same remark. In order, therefore, to show that critical value-judgements are all ultimately related to choices, and would not be made if they were not so related, we require to ask, for what purpose we have standards.

It has been pointed out by Mr. Urmson that we do not speak generally of 'good' wireworms. This is because we never have any occasion for choosing between wireworms, and therefore require no guidance in so doing. We therefore need to have no standards for wireworms. But it is easy to imagine circumstances in which this situation might alter. Suppose that wireworms came into use as a special kind of bait for fishermen. Then we might speak of having dug up a very good wireworm (one, for example, that was exception- ally fat and attractive to fish), just as now, no doubt, sea- fishermen might talk of having dug up a very good lug-worm. We only have standards for a class of objects, we only talk of the virtues of one specimen as against another, we only use value-words about them, when occasions are known to exist, or are conceivable, in which we, or someone else, would have to choose between specimens. We should not call pictures good or bad if no one ever had the choice of seeing them or not seeing them (or of studying them or not studying them in the way that art students study pictures, or of buying them or not buying them). Lest, by the way, I should seem to have introduced a certain vagueness by specifying so many alter- native kinds of choices, it must be pointed out that the matter can, if desired, be made as precise as we require; for we can specify, when we have called a picture a good one, within what class we have called it good; for example, we can say 'I meant a good picture to study, but not to buy'.

Some further examples may be given. We should not speak of good sunsets, unless sometimes the decision had to be made, whether to go to the window to look at the sunset; we should not speak of good billiard-cues, unless sometimes we had to choose one billiard-cue in preference to another; we should not speak of good men unless we had the choice, what sort of men to try to become. Leibniz, when he spoke of 'the best of all possible worlds', had in mind a creator choosing between the possibilities. The choice that is envisaged need not ever occur, nor even be expected ever to occur; it is enough for it to be envisaged as occurring, in order that we should be able to make a value-judgement with reference to it. It must be admitted, however, that the most useful value-judgements are those which have reference to choices that we might very likely have to make.

8. 2. It should be pointed out that even judgements about past choices do not refer merely to the past. As we shall see, all value-judgements are covertly universal in character, which is the same as to say that they refer to, and express acceptance of, a standard which has an application to other similar instances. If I censure someone for having done something, I envisage the possibility of him, or someone else, or myself, having to make a similar choice again; otherwise there would be no point in censuring him. Thus, if I say to a man whom I am teaching to drive 'You did that manœuvre badly' this is a very typical piece of driving-instruction; and driving-instruction consists in teaching a man to drive not in the past but in the future; to this end we censure or commend past pieces of driving, in order to impart to him the standard which is to guide him in his subsequent conduct.

When we commend an object, our judgement is not solely about that particular object, but is inescapably about objects like it. Thus, if I say that a certain motor-car is a good one, I am not merely saying something about that particular motor-car. To say something about that particular car, merely, would not be to commend. To commend, as we have seen, is to guide choices. Now for guiding a particular choice we have a linguistic instrument which is not that of commendation, namely, the singular imperative. If I wish merely to tell someone to choose a particular car, with no thought of the kind of car to which it belongs, I can say 'Take that one'. If instead of this I say 'That is a good one', I am saying something more. I am implying that if any motor-car were just like that one, it would be a good one too; whereas by saying 'Take that one', I do not imply that, if my hearer sees another car just like that one, he is to take it too. But further, the implication of the judgement 'That is a good motor-car' does not extend merely to motor-cars *exactly* like that one.

If this were so, the implication would be for practical purposes useless; for nothing is exactly like anything else. It extends to every motor-car that is like that one in the *relevant* particulars; and the relevant particulars are its virtues—those of its characteristics for which I was commending it, or which I was calling good about it. Whenever we commend, we have in mind something about the object commended which is the reason for our commendation. It therefore always makes sense, after someone has said 'That is a good motor-car', to ask 'What is good about it?' or 'Why do you call it good?' or 'What features of it are you commending?' It may not always be easy to answer this question precisely, but it is always a legitimate question. If we did not understand why it was always a legitimate question, we should not understand the way in which the word 'good' functions.

We may illustrate this point by comparing two dialogues (similar to the one in 5. 2):

(1) *X.* Jones' motor-car is a good one.

 Y. What makes you call it good?

 X. Oh, just that it's good.

 Y. But there must be some *reason* for your calling it good, I mean some property that it has in virtue of which you call it good.

 X. No; the property in virtue of which I call it good is just its goodness and nothing else.

 Y. But do you mean that its shape, speed, weight, manœuvrability &c., are irrelevant to whether you call it good or not?

 X. Yes, quite irrelevant; the only relevant property is that of goodness, just as, if I called it yellow, the only relevant property would be that of yellowness.

(2) The same dialogue, only with 'yellow' substituted for 'good' and 'yellowness' for 'goodness' throughout, and the last clause ('just as . . . yellowness') omitted.

The reason why X's position in the first dialogue is eccentric is that since, as we have already remarked, 'good' is a 'super-venient' or 'consequential' epithet, one may always legitimately be asked when one has called something a good something, 'What is good about it?' Now to answer this question is to give the properties in virtue of which we call it good. Thus, if I have said, 'That is a good motor-car' and someone asks 'Why? What is good about it?' and I reply 'Its high speed combined with its stability on the road', I indicate that I call it good in virtue of its having these properties or virtues. Now to do this is *eo ipso* to say something about other motor-cars which have these properties. If any motor-car whatever had these properties, I should have, if I were not to be inconsistent, to agree that it was, *pro tanto*, a good motor-car; though of course it might, although it had these properties in its favour, have other countervailing disadvantages, and so be, taken all in all, not a good motor-car.

This last difficulty can always be got over by specifying in detail why I called the first motor-car a good one. Suppose that a second motor-car were like the first one in speed and stability, but gave its passengers no protection from the rain, and proved difficult to get into and out of. I should not then call it a good motor-car, although it had those characteristics which led me to call the first one good. This shows that I should not have called the first one good either, if it too had had the bad characteristics of the second one; and so in specifying what was good about the first one, I ought to have added '. . . and the protection it gives to the passengers and the ease with which one can get into and out of it'. This process could be repeated indefinitely until I had given a complete list of the characteristics of the first motor-car which were required to make me allow it to be a good one. This, in itself, would not be saying all that there was to be said about my standards for judging motor-cars—for there might be other motor-cars which, although falling short to a certain extent in these characteristics, had other countervailing good characteristics; for example, soft upholstery, large accommodation, or small consumption of petrol. But it would be at any rate some help to my hearer in building up an idea of my standards in motor-cars; and in this lies the importance of such questions and answers, and the importance of recognizing their relevance, whenever a value-judgement has been made. For one of the purposes of making such judgements is to make known the standard.

When I commend a motor-car I am guiding the choices of my hearer not merely in relation to that particular motor-car but in relation to motor-cars in general. What I have said to him will be of assistance to him whenever in the future he has to choose a motor-car or advise anyone else on the choice of a motor-car or even design a motor-car (choose what sort of motor-car to have made) or write a general treatise on the design of motor-cars (which involves choosing what sort of motor-cars to advise other people to have made). The method whereby I give him this assistance is by making known to him a standard for judging motor-cars.

This process has, as we have noticed, certain features in common with the process of defining (making known the meaning or application of) a descriptive word, though there are important differences. We have now to notice a further resemblance between showing the usage of a word and showing how to choose between motor-cars. In neither case can the instruction be done successfully unless the instructor is consistent in his teaching. If I use 'red' for objects of a wide variety of colours, my hearer will never learn from me a consistent usage of the word. Similarly, if I commend motor-cars with widely different or even contrary characteristics, what I say to him will not be of assistance to him in choosing motor-cars subsequently, because I am not teaching him any consistent standard—or any standard at all, for a standard is by definition consistent. He will say, 'I don't see by what standards you are judging these motor-cars; please explain to

me why you call them all good, although they are so different'.
Of course, I might be able to give a satisfactory explanation.
I might say, 'There are different sorts of motor-cars, each
good in its way; there are sports cars, whose prime requisites
are speed and manœuvrability; and family cars, which ought
rather to be capacious and economical; and taxis, and so on.
So when I say a car is good which is fast and manœuvrable,
although it is neither capacious nor economical, you must
understand that I am commending it as a sports car, not as
a family car'. But suppose that I did not recognize the relevance of his question; suppose that I was just doling out the
predicate 'good' entirely haphazard, as the whim took me.
It is clear that in this case I should teach him no standard
at all.

We thus have to distinguish two questions that can always
be asked in elucidation of a judgement containing the word
'good'. Suppose that someone says 'That is a good one'. We
can then always ask (1) 'Good what—sports car or family car
or taxi or example to quote in a logic-book?' Or we can ask
(2) 'What makes you call it good?' To ask the first question
is to ask for the class within which evaluative comparisons are
being made. Let us call it the class of comparison. To ask the
second question is to ask for the virtues or 'good-making
characteristics'. These two questions are, however, not independent; for what distinguishes the class of comparison
'sports car' from the class 'family car' is the set of virtues
which are to be looked for in the respective classes. This is
so in all cases where the class of comparison is defined by
means of a functional word—for obviously 'sports car',
'family car', and 'taxi' are functional to a very much higher
degree than plain 'motor-car'. Sometimes, however, a class
of comparison may be further specified without making it
more functional; for example, in explaining the phrase 'good
wine' we might say 'I mean good wine for this district, not
good wine compared with all the wines that there are'.

8. 3. Now since it is the purpose of the word 'good' and other value-words to be used for teaching standards, their logic is in accord with this purpose. We are therefore in a position at last to explain the feature of the word 'good' which I pointed out at the beginning of this investigation. The reason why I cannot apply the word 'good' to one picture, if I refuse to apply it to another picture which I agree to be in all other respects exactly similar, is that by doing this I should be defeating the purpose for which the word is designed. I should be commending one object, and so purporting to teach my hearers one standard, while in the same breath refusing to commend a similar object, and so undoing the lesson just imparted. By seeking to impart two inconsistent standards, I should be imparting no standard at all. The effect of such an utterance is similar to that of a contradiction; for in a contradiction, I say two inconsistent things, and so the effect is that the hearer does not know what I am trying to say.

What I have said so far may also be put into another terminology, that of principles, which we were using in Part I. To teach a person—or to decide on for oneself—a standard for judging the merits of objects of a certain class is to teach or decide on principles for choosing between objects of that class. To know the principles for choosing motor-cars is to be able to judge between motor-cars or to tell a good one from a bad one. If I say 'That isn't a good motor-car' and am asked what virtue it is, the lack of which makes me say this, and reply 'It isn't stable on the road', then I am appealing to a principle.

In view of the close similarity in purpose between value-judgements and principles for choosing, it is interesting to notice that the characteristic of value-judgements which we are discussing (their necessity for consistency with one another) is shared by universal imperative sentences, as indeed by all universal sentences. We have seen that I cannot say 'This is a good motor-car, but the one next to it, though exactly like it in all other respects, is not good'. For the same reason, we cannot say 'If you can, always choose a motor-car like this one, but do not always choose a motor-car like the one next to it, which is exactly like this one'. This sentence is self-contradictory, because it enjoins the hearer both, always to choose a motor-car like this one, and, not always to choose a motor-car like this one. A similar contradiction in the indicative mood would be 'Animals like this one are always barren, but animals like the one next to it, which is exactly like this one, are not always barren'

This connexion between value-judgements and principles helps us to answer the question posed at the beginning of this chapter. What I said in the previous chapter about the relation of the evaluative to the descriptive meaning of 'good', and the way in which standards are adopted and changed, is readily accounted for when we realize that the context in which we use these words is the context of decisions of principle such as were discussed in 4. 2. A value-judgement may stand in a variety of relations to the standard to which it refers. In virtue of its descriptive meaning it informs the hearer that the object conforms to the standard. This is true even if the judgement is an 'inverted-commas' or a conventional one. Most of the complexity of the relation is due, however, to the evaluative meaning. If the standard is one that is well-known and generally accepted, the value-judgement may do no more than express the speaker's acceptance of or adherence to it (though it never *states that* he accepts or adheres to it; for this we have other expressions, such as 'It is my view that, to be good, a strawberry should have firm flesh'). If the hearer is someone not acquainted with the standard (e.g. a child) the function of the value-judgement may be also to acquaint him with it or teach it to him. If we do this, we are not merely informing him that the standard is of such and such a kind; we are instructing him to make his future choices on a certain principle. We do this by pointing out to him examples of objects that do and do not conform to the standard, and saying 'That is a good X', 'That is a bad X', &c. If the standard to which we refer is either one for objects of a class which have not previously been placed in order of merit (such as cacti), or if we are consciously advocating a standard which is at variance with the received one, then our purpose is almost entirely prescriptive; we are actually setting up a new standard or modifying an accepted one. Suppose, for example, that I said 'The *Highway Code* says that it is good driving to give a multiplicity of signals; but really it is better to give fewer signals, look carefully to see that you are not obstructing other vehicles, and always drive in such a way that your intended movements are obvious without signals'; I should be prescribing, not informing.[1] I may, moreover, say this sort of thing to myself in the course of acquiring driving skill; this is like self-teaching. We thus see that the language of values is admirably suited for the expression of everything that we require to say in the course of either deciding on or instructing in or modifying principles; thus the whole of Chapter 4 might have been couched, not in terms of universal imperative principles, but of value-judgements. That is why the logic of value-judgements cannot be understood unless we have first made ourselves familiar with such contexts.

[1] See *The Autocar*, 17 Aug. 1951, Editorial.

9

'GOOD' IN MORAL CONTEXTS

9. 1. IT is time now to ask whether 'good', as used in moral contexts, has any of the features to which I have drawn attention in non-moral ones. It will no doubt be thought by some readers that all that I have said hitherto is entirely irrelevant to ethics. To think this is to miss the enlightenment of some very interesting parallels; but I have no right on my part to assume that 'good' behaves in at all the fashion that I have described when it is used in morals. To this problem we must now address ourselves; but first something more must be said about another distinction of which I may seem to have made light, that between the so-called 'intrinsic' and 'instrumental' uses of 'good'.

There has been a disposition among philosophers to do one of two opposite things. The first is to suppose that all value-judgements whatever relate to the performance by an object of a function distinct from the object itself. The second is to suppose that, because there are some objects which are commended for their own sakes, and do not have an obvious function beyond their mere existence, to commend such an object is to do something quite different from commending an object which does have a function. It will help us to avoid doing either of these things if we avail ourselves of the general notions of 'virtue' and 'standard' which I have been using in the preceding chapters.

When we are dealing with objects which are evaluated solely in virtue of their performance of a function, the virtues of such objects will consist in those characteristics which either promote, or themselves constitute, the good performance of the function. The matter can be made clear by supposing that what we are judging is the *performance* of the object, not the object itself. Imagine that we are judging a fire-extinguisher. To do so we watch it being used to put out a fire, and then judge its performance. Certain characteristics of the performance count as virtues (e.g. putting out the fire quickly, causing little damage to property, emitting no dangerous fumes, small consumption of expensive chemicals, &c.). Note that certain of the expressions used in specifying the standard (e.g. 'damage' and 'dangerous') are themselves value-expressions; these indicate that the specification of the standard is not in itself complete, but includes 'cross-references' to standards for evaluating, respectively, the state of repair of property, and the effect of gases on the human body. It would be impossible to specify the standard completely without having for purposes of reference a specification of all the other standards to which it is necessary to refer. Aristotle[1] gives examples of such cross-references in which the standards are arranged hierarchically, the cross-references being all in the same direction. It does not seem obvious that they need be so arranged, though it would be tidy if they were.

Now what we must notice, for our present purposes, about the above list of virtues of the fire-extinguisher's performance, is that it is just a list of virtues, not differing logically from the list of virtues of a class of objects not having a function. Compare it, for example, with the list of virtues of a good bath. A good bath is good both instrumentally (in that it is conducive to cleanliness) and intrinsically (for we should not have nearly so many baths if our only purpose in having them were to become clean). Let us for the moment ignore the instrumental goodness of the bath, and concentrate on its intrinsic goodness. To be good intrinsically, a bath must be within a certain range of temperature, which must be maintained throughout its duration; the vessel must be above a certain minimum size, which varies with that of the bather; it must

---

[1] *Nicomachean Ethics*, I. i. 2.

be of a certain shape; and it must be full of soft clean water; there must be soap above a certain degree of fineness (e.g. not containing abrasives or free caustics)—and the reader may add to the list according to his taste. In this specification I have tried to avoid cross-references to other standards, but I have not been entirely successful; e.g., 'clean water' means 'water in which there is no dirt', and what is to count as dirt is a matter for evaluation. Thus even where we are dealing with intrinsic goodness we cannot avoid cross-references, and therefore it is not the necessity for cross-references which makes goodness instrumental.

We notice that in both cases—the fire-extinguisher and the bath—we have a standard or list of virtues, and commend objects which possess these virtues. In the case of the fire-extinguisher we commend directly its performance, and the object only indirectly; in the case of the bath we might be said to commend the object directly. But this is really a distinction without a difference; are we to say that 'inducing heat in my skin' is a performance of the bath, or are we to say that 'being hot' is a quality of the bath? Similarly, one of the virtues required in a good pineapple is that it should be sweet; is its sweetness an intrinsic quality of the pineapple, or is it the disposition to produce certain desirable sensations in me? When we can answer such questions, we shall be able to draw a precise distinction between intrinsic and instrumental goodness.

It would, however, be a mistake to say that there is *no* difference between what we do when we commend a fire-extinguisher and what we do when we commend a sunset. We commend them for entirely different reasons, and in the case of the fire-extinguisher these reasons all refer to what it is intended to do. We saw above that if 'good' is followed by a functional word (e.g. the name of an instrument), this word itself gives us a partial specification of the virtues required; whereas in other cases this specification is absent. All that I am maintaining is that the logical apparatus of virtues and standards which I have been elaborating is sufficiently general to cover both instrumental and intrinsic goodness. And to see this is to make the first step towards seeing that it may be general enough to cover moral goodness too. To this question we must now turn.

9. 2. Let us review some of the reasons that have led people to hold that the use of the word 'good' in moral contexts is totally different from its use in non-moral ones. The first reason is connected with the difference between intrinsic and instrumental good, and we have already dealt with it. The second reason is that the properties which make a man morally good are obviously different from those which make a chronometer good. It is therefore easy to think that the *meaning* of the word 'good' is different in the two cases. But this can now be seen to be a mistaken conclusion. The descriptive meaning is certainly different, as the descriptive meaning of 'good' in 'good apple' is different from its meaning in 'good cactus'; but the evaluative meaning is the same —in both cases we are commending. We are commending as a man, not as a chronometer. If we insisted on calling the meaning of 'good' different, because the virtues required in objects of different classes are different, we should end up with what Mr. Urmson calls 'a homonym with as many punning meanings as the situations it applied to'.[1]

The third reason is this: it is felt that somehow 'moral goodness' is more august, more important, and therefore deserves to have a logic all its own. This plea seldom comes out into the open; but it lies behind much of the argument, and in itself has something to recommend it. We do attach more importance to a man's being a good man than to a chronometer's being a good chronometer. We do not *blame* chronometers for being bad (though we do blame their makers). We get stirred up about moral goodness in a way

---

[1] *Mind*, lix (1950), 161 (also in *Logic and Language*, ii, ed. Flew, 176).

that few people get stirred up about technical or other sorts of goodness. This is why many readers will have been irritated by my supposing that the behaviour of 'good' in 'good sewage effluent' can have any interest for the moral philosopher. We have to ask, therefore, why it is that we feel this way, and whether the fact that we do makes it necessary for us to give an entirely different account of the logic of 'good' in the two cases.

We get stirred up about the goodness of men because we are men. This means that the acceptance of a judgement, that such and such a man's act is good in circumstances of a certain sort, involves the acceptance of the judgement that it would be good, were we ourselves placed in similar circumstances, to do likewise. And since we might *be* placed in similar circumstances, we feel deeply about the question. We feel less deeply, it must be admitted, about the question, whether it was a bad act of Agamemnon to sacrifice Iphigenia, than about the question, whether it was a bad act of Mrs. Smith to travel on the railway without paying her fare; for we are not likely to be in Agamemnon's position, but most of us travel on railways. Acceptance of a moral judgement about Mrs. Smith's act is likely to have a closer bearing upon our future conduct than acceptance of one about Agamemnon's. But we never envisage ourselves turning into chronometers.

These observations are to a certain extent confirmed by the behaviour of technicians and artists. As Hesiod pointed out, these people do get stirred up about their respective non-moral goodnesses, in the way that ordinary people get stirred up about moral questions: 'Potters get angry with potters, and carpenters with carpenters, and beggars with beggars, and poets with poets'.[1] Commercial competition is not the only reason—for it is possible to compete without malice. When an architect, for example, says of another architect's house, with feeling, 'That is a thoroughly badly designed

[1] *Works and Days*, 25.

house', the reason for the feeling is that if he were to admit that the house was well designed, he would be admitting that in avoiding in his own work features like those of the design in question, he had been wrong; and this might mean altering his whole way of designing houses, which would be painful.

Further, we cannot get out of being men, as we can get out of being architects or out of making or using chronometers. Since this is so, there is no avoiding the (often painful) consequences of abiding by the moral judgements that we make. The architect who was forced to admit that a rival's house was better than anything he had ever produced or could produce, might be upset; but in the last resort he could become a barman instead. But if I admit that the life of St. Francis was morally better than mine, and really mean this as an evaluation, there is nothing for it but to try to be more like St. Francis, which is arduous. That is why most of our 'moral judgements about the saints are merely conventional—we never intend them to be a guide in determining our own conduct.

Moreover, in the case of differences about morals it is very difficult, and, in cases where the effect on our own life is profound, impossible, to say 'It's all a matter of taste; let's agree to differ'; for to agree to differ is only possible when we can be sure that we shall not be forced to make choices which will radically affect the choices of other people. This is especially true where choices have to be made co-operatively; it must be pointed out, however, that though most moral choices are of this kind, this sort of situation is not peculiar to morals. The members of the Kon-tiki expedition could not have agreed to differ about how to build their raft, and families sharing a kitchen cannot agree to differ about its organization. But although we can usually get out of building rafts or sharing kitchens, we cannot easily get out of living in societies with other people. Perhaps men living in complete isolation could agree to differ about morals.

It would at any rate seem that communities not in close con-
tact with one another could agree to differ about some moral
questions without actual inconvenience. To say this, of
course, is not necessarily to maintain any kind of moral
relativism, for communities could agree to differ about whether the earth was round. To agree to differ is to say, in effect,
'We will differ about this question, but let us not be angry or
fight about it'; it is not to say 'we will differ, but let us not
differ'; for the latter would be a logical impossibility. And so
if two communities agreed to differ about, say, the moral
desirability of legalized gambling in their respective terri-
tories, what would happen would be this; they would say 'We
will continue to hold, one of us that it is wrong to legalize
gambling, and the other that it is not wrong; but we will not
get angry about each other's laws, or seek to interfere in each
other's administration of them'. And the same thing might
be done about other matters than gambling, provided that
what each community did had slight effect outside its own
borders. Such agreements will not work, however, if one
community holds it to be a moral duty to prevent certain
practices taking place wherever they occur.

Such a case is worth considering in order to contrast with
it the more usual state of affairs; normally the moral judgements that we make, and hold to, deeply affect the lives of our
neighbours; and this in itself is enough to explain the peculiar
place that we assign to them. If we add to this the logical point,
already mentioned, that moral judgements always have a
possible bearing on our own conduct, in that we cannot in
the fullest sense accept them without conforming to them
(that this is a tautology will appear in 11. 2), then no further
explanation is needed of the special status of morals. This
special status does not require a special logic to back it up; it
results from the fact that we are using the ordinary apparatus
of value-language in order to commend or condemn the most
intimate actions of ourselves and those like us. We may add

that the 'emotivity' of much moral utterance, which some have thought to be of the essence of evaluative language, is only a symptom—and a most unreliable one—of an evaluative use of words. Moral language is frequently emotive, simply because the situations in which it is typically used are situations about which we often feel deeply. One of the chief uses of the comparison which I have been drawing between moral and non-moral value-language is to make it clear that the essential logical features of value-words can be present where the emotions are not markedly involved.

It might be objected that my account of the matter gives no means of distinguishing prudential judgements like 'It is never a good thing to volunteer for anything in the Army' from properly moral judgements like 'It is not good to break one's promises'. But the considerations given earlier (8. 2) enable us to distinguish satisfactorily between these two classes of judgement. It is clear from the context that in the second case we are commending within a different class of comparison, and requiring a different set of virtues. Sometimes we commend an act within the class of acts having an effect upon the agent's future happiness; sometimes we commend an act within the class of acts indicative of his moral character, that is to say, those acts which show whether or not he is a good man—and the class of comparison 'man' in this context is the class 'man to try to become like' (12. 3). Which of these we are doing is always clear from the context, and there is nearly always a further verbal difference too, as in the example quoted. It must be admitted, however, that a great deal of research has still to be done on the different classes of comparison within which we commend people and acts.

When we use the word 'good' in order to commend morally, we are always directly or indirectly commending *people*. Even when we use the expression 'good act' or others like it, the reference is indirectly to human characters. This, as has often been pointed out, constitutes a difference between the words 'good' and 'right'. In speaking, therefore, of moral goodness, I shall speak only of the expression 'good man' and similar expressions. We have to consider whether in fact this expression has the same logical features as the non-moral uses of 'good' which we have been discussing, remembering that clearly 'man' in 'good man' is not normally a functional word, and never so when moral commendation is being given.

9. 3. First, let us take that characteristic of 'good' which has been called its supervenience. Suppose that we say 'St. Francis was a good man'. It is logically impossible to say this and to maintain at the same time that there might have been another man placed in precisely the same circumstances as St. Francis, and who behaved in them in exactly the same way, but who differed from St. Francis in this respect only, that he was not a good man. I am supposing, of course, that the judgement is made in both cases upon the whole life of the subject, 'inner' and overt. This example is similar in the relevant particulars to that in 5. 2.

Next, the explanation of this logical impossibility does not lie in any form of naturalism; it is not the case that there is any conjunction C of descriptive characteristics such that to say that a man has C entails that he is morally good. For, if this were the case, we should be unable to commend any man for having those characteristics; we should only be able to say that he had them. Nevertheless, the judgement that a man is morally good is not logically independent of the judgement that he has certain other characteristics which we may call virtues or good-making characteristics; there is a relation between them, although it is not one of entailment or of identity of meaning.

Our previous discussion of non-moral goodness helps us to understand what the relation is. It is that a statement of the characteristics of the man (the minor or factual premiss) *together with* a specification of a standard for judging men morally (the major premiss), entails a moral judgement upon him. And moral standards have many of the features that we have found in other value-standards. 'Good', as used in morals, has a descriptive and an evaluative meaning, and the latter is primary. To know the descriptive meaning is to know by what standards the speaker is judging. Let us take a case where the standard is well known. If a parson says of a girl that she is a good girl, we can form a shrewd idea, of what description she is; we may expect her to go to church, for example. It is therefore easy to fall into the error of supposing that by calling her a good girl the parson means simply that she has these descriptive characteristics.

It is quite true that part of what the parson means is that the girl has these characteristics; but it is to be hoped that this is not all he means. He also means to commend her for having them; and this part of his meaning is primary. The reason why we know, when a parson says a girl is good, what sort of girl she is, how she normally behaves, &c., is that parsons are usually consistent in the way they award commendation. It is through being used consistently by parsons for commending certain sorts of behaviour in girls that the word comes to have a descriptive force.

To this unkind parody may be added another. If two Indian Army majors of the old school had been talking about a new arrival in the Mess, and one of them had said 'He's an awfully good man', we could have guessed that the subaltern referred to played polo, stuck pigs with *élan*, and was not on familiar terms with educated Indians. The remark, therefore, would have conveyed information to one versed in the culture of British India. It would have been informative, because officers of the Indian Army were accustomed to award commendation or the reverse according to consistent standards. But it cannot have been informative in the beginning. The standard must have got established by some pioneer evaluators; when the Indian Army was young there was no established standard for the behaviour of subalterns. The standard became established by officers making commendatory judgements which were not statements of fact or informative in the least, to the effect that it was the mark of a good man, for example, to play polo. For these pioneers, the sentence 'Plunkett is a good man' did not in any way entail the sentence 'Plunkett plays polo' or vice versa. The former was an expression of commendation, the latter a statement of fact. But we may suppose that, after generations of officers had always commended people who played polo, it came to be assumed that, if an officer said that another officer was a good man, he must mean that, among other things, he played polo; and so the word 'good', as used by Indian Army officers, came to be, to this extent, descriptive, without in the least losing its primary evaluative meaning.

Of course, the evaluative meaning might get lost, or at least wear thin. It is of the essence of a standard to be stable; but the perpetual danger is that stability may harden to over-rigidity and ossification. It is possible to lay too much stress on the descriptive force and too little on the evaluative; standards only remain current when those who make judgements in accordance with them are quite sure that, whatever else they may be doing, they are evaluating (i.e. really seeking to guide conduct). Suppose that the Indian Army comes to be unable to use the words 'good man' in any other way than descriptively, to mean 'man who plays polo, &c.'; they will then have fallen into a kind of naive naturalism, and will be unable to commend subalterns for playing polo; and this means that they will not be able to hand on to new generations of officers their established standards. If a new subaltern has had, before his posting, the standards of a bank clerk with a timid interest in pink politics, those are the standards which he will continue to have; for his superior officers will have lost the linguistic means of teaching him any others. And even if the older officers are themselves using the word 'good' evaluatively, the extreme descriptive rigidity of their standards may lead the new subaltern to understand the word, as they use it, descriptively. This is how value-words get into inverted commas.

9. 4. That the descriptive meaning of the word 'good' is in morals, as elsewhere, secondary to the evaluative, may be seen in the following example. Let us suppose that a missionary, armed with a grammar book, lands on a cannibal island. The vocabulary of his grammar book gives him the equivalent, in the cannibals' language, of the English word 'good'. Let us suppose that, by a queer coincidence, the word is 'good'. And let us suppose, also, that it really is the equivalent—that it is, as the *Oxford English Dictionary* puts it, 'the most general adjective of commendation' in their language. If the missionary has mastered his vocabulary, he can, *so long as he uses the word evaluatively and not descriptively*, communicate with them about morals quite happily. They know that when he uses the word he is commending the person or object that he applies it to. The only thing they will find odd is that he applies it to such unexpected people, people who are meek and gentle and do not collect large quantities of scalps; whereas they themselves are accustomed to commend people who are bold and burly and collect more scalps than the average. But they and the missionary are under no misapprehension about the meaning, in the evaluative sense, of the word 'good'; it is the word one uses for commending. If they were under such a misapprehension, moral communication between them would be impossible.

We thus have a situation which would appear paradoxical to someone who thought that 'good' (either in English or in the cannibals' language) was a quality-word like 'red'. Even if the qualities in people which the missionary commended had nothing in common with the qualities which the cannibals commended, yet they would both know what the word 'good' meant. If 'good' were like 'red', this would be impossible; for then the cannibals' word and the English word would not be synonymous. If this were so, then when the missionary said that people who collected no scalps were good (English), and the cannibals said that people who collected a lot of scalps were good (cannibal), they would not be disagreeing, because in English (at any rate missionary English), 'good' would mean among other things 'doing no murder', whereas in the cannibals' language 'good' would mean something quite different, among other things 'productive of maximum scalps'. It is because in its primary evaluative meaning 'good' means neither of these things, but is in both languages the most general adjective of commendation, that the missionary can use it to teach the cannibals Christian morals.

Suppose, however, that the missionary's mission is successful. Then, the former cannibals will come to commend the same qualities in people as the missionary, and the words 'good man' will come to have a more or less common descriptive meaning. The danger will then be that the cannibals may, after a generation or two, think that that is the only sort of meaning they have. 'Good' will in that case mean for them simply 'doing what it says in the Sermon on the Mount'; and they may come to forget that it is a word of commendation; they will not realize that opinions about moral goodness have a bearing on what they themselves are to *do*. Their standards will then be in mortal danger. A Communist, landing on the island to convert the people to *his* way of life, may even take advantage of the ossification of their standards. He may say 'All these "good" Christians—missionaries and colonial servants and the rest—are just deceiving you to their own profit'. This would be to use the word descriptively with a dash of irony; and he could not do this plausibly unless the standards of the Christians had become considerably ossified. Some of the ploys of Thrasymachus in the first book of Plato's *Republic* are very similar to this.

If the reader will turn back to 4. 6 he will see that such vicissitudes of the word 'good' reflect accurately the sort of moral development there described. Moral principles or standards are first established; then they get too rigid, and the words used in referring to them become too dominantly descriptive; their evaluative force has to be painfully revived before the standards are out of danger. In the course of revival, the standards get adapted to changed circumstances; moral reform takes place, and its instrument is the evaluative use of value-language. The remedy, in fact, for moral stagnation and decay is to learn to use our value-language for the purpose for which it is designed; and this involves not merely a lesson in talking, but a lesson in doing that which we commend; for unless we are prepared to do this we are doing no more than pay lip-service to a conventional standard.

PART III

'OUGHT'

'We are discussing no trivial matter, but how
we ought to live.'
PLATO, *Republic*, 352 d

10

'OUGHT' AND 'RIGHT'

10. 1. I HAVE so far, in discussing the words used in moral discourse, confined myself largely to the word 'good', because
the characteristics to which I wished to draw attention are
most easily illustrated by the behaviour of that word. It is
necessary, however, to give some account of other words used
in moral discourse, or at any rate the more general of them;
and this is made more urgent by the fact that some moral
philosophers have drawn a very rigid distinction between
'good' and other moral words such as 'right', 'ought', and
'duty'. We shall see that it is important to draw this distinction, but that this does not prevent us giving an account of
the logical relation, which undoubtedly exists, between 'good'
and other moral words; and in this part of our inquiry, as in
others, the parallelism between moral and non-moral uses of
these words will be of assistance.

No one with the least familiarity with their uses could hold
that 'right' and 'good', for example, mean the same in any
of their contexts. To begin with, there are important differences in their grammatical behaviour. We talk of 'a good X'
but of 'the right X'; and in general we think it quite natural
to speak of there being a large number of good X's, but odd
(in most contexts) to speak of there being a large number of
right X's—though of course we may speak of there being a

large number of X's that are quite all right. It is not, therefore, surprising that 'right' has in modern English no comparative and superlative, whereas 'good' has. There are also
many nouns which 'good' can qualify, and 'right' cannot, and
vice versa. Thus we can speak of 'good art', but not of 'right
art', and of 'good batting', but not of 'right batting'; and on
the other hand, we can say 'You didn't play the right note', but
'good' could not be substituted. As the work of Professor J. L.
Austin has taught all who have had the benefit of instruction
in his methods, such peculiarities may be—though they are
not always—indicative of underlying logical differences.

On the other hand, it is also true that there are many kinds
of context in which we can use expressions containing either
of these words for much the same sort of purpose. Thus in
teaching someone to drive I may, if he fails to execute a
manœuvre to my satisfaction, say 'You didn't do that very
well' or 'You didn't do that quite right', without much distinction of meaning. Even in this context, however, there are
differences; I might say 'You did that quite well, but it wasn't
yet quite right'. The occurrence of both words in this sort
of context should incline us to think that some, at any rate,
of the things which I have said about the prescriptive function of 'good' may be applicable also to 'right', though we
shall expect also to find differences.

The same sort of distinctions can be drawn between the
words 'good' and 'ought'. These also can be used in very
similar contexts, though there are also differences. We can
say 'You ought to have let the clutch in more gently' or 'It
would have been better if you had let the clutch in more
gently'; and we can say 'You didn't do that at all well' or
'You didn't do that at all as you ought'. On the other hand,
we can say 'You did that quite well, but not yet quite as you
ought'. In general, 'ought' behaves more like 'right' than it
does like 'good'; and we shall find when we come to state
more precisely the logical relations between the three words,

that, whereas the relations between 'right' and 'ought' can be characterized comparatively simply, those between 'good' and 'ought' are much more indirect.

10. 2. In spite of these differences, there are sufficient similarities between the words 'good', 'right', and 'ought' for us to classify them all as value-words. To illustrate these similarities it will be sufficient to draw attention to the way in which the chief characteristics of 'good' which we have already noticed are also present in 'right' and 'ought'. First of all let me show that 'right' and 'ought' share what I have called the 'supervenient' character of 'good'. I will take a moral and a non-moral example of each word. If I said 'Smith acted rightly in giving her the money, but he might have given her the money, and in all other respects acted similarly, except that his act was not right', I should invite the comment 'But how could the rightness of Smith's act disappear like this? If the act, motives, circumstances, &c., were all the same, then you would be bound, logically, to judge it right in the hypothetical case as you did in the actual case. The actual action couldn't have been right and the hypothetical action not right, unless there had been *some* other difference between the actions, or their circumstances, or their motives, or something else'. Actions cannot differ only as regards their rightness, any more than pictures or anything else can differ only as regards their goodness; and this impossibility is a logical one, stemming from the way in which, and the purposes for which, we use these words.

Similarly, we cannot say, 'You changed gear that time at absolutely the right moment; but you might have changed it at the same moment, and all the other circumstances might have been the same, only it might not have been the right moment'. This shows that this characteristic is not peculiar to moral uses of the word. And similarly with 'ought'; I cannot say 'Smith ought to have given her the money, but this might not have been so although everything else might have been the same'; and I cannot say 'You ought to have changed gear sooner, but this might not have been so, although everything else might have been the same'.

I have already hinted why we cannot say this sort of thing; it has to do with the covert universality of sentences containing these words. Let us, however, notice briefly that the reason is not, as might be thought, that sentences containing the words 'right' or 'ought' or their opposites are *entailed* by any set of sentences setting out in descriptive terms the facts or circumstances to which we are referring. With 'ought' it would be most implausible to maintain this. If it were so, then, to take a particular example, 'You ought to change down when changing down would enable the engine to run more smoothly' might be entailed by the analytic sentence 'Changing down would enable the engine to run more smoothly when it would enable the engine to run more smoothly', and might therefore be itself analytic, which in ordinary usage it is not. It is a *reason* for changing down that this would enable the engine to run more smoothly; but the fact that it would enable the engine to run more smoothly does not entail (i.e. allow us to infer in virtue solely of its meaning) that we ought to change down. And the same is true of whatever other factual sentence we may choose, and for all prescriptive uses of the word 'ought'. Thus if a writer on mothercraft informs us that to say that a baby ought to be of a certain weight *means the same* as to say that that is the mean of the observed weights of a random sample of babies of the same age, we shall be on our guard.

With 'right', the danger of naturalism is perhaps more insidious; but by this time we should be immune to it. If 'Now is the right time to change gear' were entailed by a descriptive sentence of the form 'Now it is the case that C', then to say 'When it is the case that C, it is the right time to change gear', would be to utter a tautology, which, whatever descriptive expression we substitute for C, it never is. And this is even more obvious in the case of moral uses. Suppose that someone were to maintain that 'It is not right to do A' is entailed by 'A has been forbidden by the ruler of our State', we should only need to point out that in that case 'It is not right to do what has been forbidden by the ruler of our State' would be entailed by the analytic sentence 'What has been forbidden by the ruler of our State has been forbidden by the ruler of our State', and would therefore be itself analytic, which in ordinary usage it is not. But it is unnecessary further to elaborate this familiar argument.

The reason, then, for the 'supervenient' character of the words 'right' and 'ought' is not of the sort that naturalism suggests. We have therefore to inquire what else could be the reason. In order to conduct this inquiry, we must first put the words in their proper linguistic setting. They are used primarily for giving advice or instruction, or in general for guiding choices. In what follows, I shall speak principally of the word 'ought'; but later we shall see that an analysis of the word 'ought' can readily be extended so as to cover the word 'right'. As with the word 'good', I shall not at first distinguish between moral and non-moral uses, but shall deal with those features that are common to both.

10. 3. The word 'ought' is used for prescribing; but since prescription can be of more than one kind, several distinctions require to be made. Suppose that someone is asking himself, or asking us, 'What shall I do?' or some other question of this general form. In order to help such a person make up his mind, we may say at least three different sorts of things. I shall distinguish them by the terms 'type A prescriptions', 'type B prescriptions', and 'type C prescriptions'. The following are examples of type A, which are singular imperatives:

A_1. Use the starting handle.

A_2. Get cushions of a different colour.

A_3. Pay him back the money.

It is characteristic of such prescriptions that they apply directly only to the occasion on which they are offered. This is not true of type B prescriptions, of which the following are examples:

B_1. If the engine fails to start at once on the self-starter, one ought always to use the starting handle.

B_2. One ought never to put magenta cushions on top of scarlet upholstery.

B_3. One ought always to pay back money which one has promised to pay back.

Type B prescriptions apply to a *kind* of occasion, rather than directly to an individual occasion. The third type of prescription is type C:

C_1. You ought to use the starting handle.

C_2. You ought to get cushions of a different colour.

C_3. You ought to pay him back the money.

A type C prescription has some of the characteristics of both types A and B: it applies directly to an individual occasion; but it also invokes or appeals to some more general type B prescription. Thus, if I say C_1, I am invoking some general principle like B_1. Of course, it might not be B_1 itself that I was invoking; it might be B_{11}—'When one's battery is at all weak, one ought always to use the starting handle', or B_{12}—'When starting from cold in the morning, one ought always to use the starting handle'. Which of these principles I am invoking could be elicited by asking the question 'Why ought I to use the starting handle?' Thus, by uttering a type C prescription we seem to imply (in a loose sense) that there is *some* principle of type B that we are invoking—though it may not be at once clear, even to us, exactly what this principle is. This is not the case with type A prescriptions; if I say A_1, I may be merely prescribing for this particular occasion (perhaps because I have thought 'Let's see if he knows how to crank a car') without any thought of there being a general principle for all occasions of this kind. It is true that if I am asked to *justify* A_1, or give reasons for it, I may appeal to a principle; but even so, type A prescriptions imply type B principles only in the minimal sense that if someone gives us such a piece of advice, we can usually assume that he can give us some general reason for it; whereas type C implies type B in the stronger sense that it would be logically illegitimate to give a type C prescription while denying that there was any principle on which it depended. By 'logically illegitimate', I mean that my usage of the word 'ought' would be so eccentric as to make people wonder what I meant by it.

It is time now to consider *post eventum* 'ought'-judgements. These are judgements of the form:

D_1. You ought to have used the starting handle.
D_2. You ought to have got cushions of a different colour.
D_3. You ought to have paid him back the money.

It is clear that these stand in the same sort of relation to type B principles as do type C prescriptions. 'You ought to have used (then) . . .' is the past tense of 'You ought to use (now) . . .'. Both depend in the same way upon 'One ought always to use . . .'. Both, moreover, have a further function; they can be used in order to *instruct* in the general rule. We learn by the process of generalization from instances; the instructor gives an example of a particular thing that we ought to have done or ought to do; and after a number of such instances have been pointed out, we learn what we ought to do in all circumstances of a given kind. The instances may be pointed out either *ante eventum*, as in 'You ought to use . . . ' or *post eventum*, as in 'You ought to have used . . .'.

When we ourselves recognize that an act which we have done conflicted with a principle which we determine to abide by, we say 'I ought not to have done that'. When we recognize that an act which we have been contemplating would be a breach of such a principle, we say 'I ought not to do that'.

In both cases, it may be the first time that we have thought about the principle—it may even be the first time that anyone has thought of the principle; the decision of principle that is expressed by this 'ought'-sentence may be an entirely new one. It is most important that we can learn without being taught.

The word 'instruct', used above, is of course somewhat too narrow. We have just seen that self-teaching is included; but even so the word 'ought' is not used only in what we may call 'instructional' situations. Suppose that I say 'They ought not to build any more by-passes round Oxford'. This depends on some such general principle as 'When traffic census figures show that all but a very small proportion of the traffic in a town is terminating traffic which could not use a bypass, large sums of money ought not to be expended on one'. We cannot, in the ordinary sense of the word, speak here of 'instructing in the general principle', for the person addressed is not likely to be my pupil. But he might be—I might be giving a lecture on the location of roads—and the other occasions on which I should use such a sentence are sufficiently similar to the instructional type of situation for the analogy to be quite obvious. In all such cases the object is to guide the actions of people in the future.

10. 4. The reasons why we have general 'ought'-principles for activities like driving, the choice of colours, road-planning, and moral behaviour are these: first, these are activities in which circumstances continually recur which force us to answer—in act if not in word—the question 'What shall I do?'; secondly, these circumstances are classifiable into kinds, the members of which are sufficiently like one another for a similar answer to be appropriate in all circumstances of the same kind; and thirdly, unless we are content to have a teacher standing by, all our lives, to tell us on every occasion just what to do, we have to learn (from others or by ourselves) principles for answering these questions. Everything that we are taught how to do must, as we have seen, be reducible to principles, though these may be 'know-hows' hard to formulate in language and more easily taught by example than by precept (4. 3).

We saw, in connexion with the word 'good', that the reason for its supervenience is that it is used in order to teach or affirm or otherwise draw attention to a standard for choosing between objects of a certain class; and that what I then said about standards could have been put instead in terms of rules or principles for choosing. It is not, therefore, surprising to find that 'ought', which is used for a very similar purpose, is subject to the same restriction. The reason why we cannot say the things which I have instanced is that to do so would be to attempt to teach or advocate two mutually inconsistent principles in the same breath.

'Ought' also shares, as we should expect, the characteristics of 'good' which concern the relations between its descriptive and evaluative or prescriptive forces. It is clear that some sentences containing the word 'ought' have descriptive force. Suppose that I say 'At the very moment when he ought to have been arriving at the play, he was grovelling underneath his car five miles away'. Here, provided that we know at what time the play began, we are as accurately informed about the time, as about the place at which he was grovelling. This is because we all accept the principle that the time at which we ought to arrive at a play (the right time to arrive) is shortly before it begins. Here too, therefore, the descriptive or informative function of 'ought'-sentences increases in direct proportion to the degree to which the principle is generally accepted or known to be accepted. But their primary function is not to give information; it is to prescribe or advise or instruct; and this function can be fulfilled when no information is being conveyed. Thus, if I am teaching a man to drive, and in particular to perform the manœuvre of getting the car in motion when it is pointing up a hill, I may say 'At the moment at which you ought to let go the hand-brake, you can hear the note of the engine drop'. This does not, as in the previous case, give him any information as to when he will hear the note of the engine drop; it rather tells him when he ought to let go the handbrake; it is used to teach him one of the rules of driving; whereas in the previous case it would have been odd if my intention had been to tell or teach anyone a rule about when one ought to turn up at the theatre.

This same feature is found in moral contexts. Suppose that I ask 'How hard is X working this term?' and get the reply 'Not as hard as he ought to be'; this answer gives me information about how hard X has been working, because I know how hard a person in X's circumstances is expected to work. If, on the other hand, I were unfamiliar with the standards of industry current (e.g. because I was a foreign student newly arrived in the country), someone might seek to apprise me of these standards by saying 'If you want to know how hard one ought to work, look at X; X is not working as hard as he ought to; so you ought to work harder than him at any rate'. This would be a predominantly prescriptive use.

10. 5. We have next to inquire whether what I have said about the alleged 'instrumental' and 'intrinsic' uses of the word 'good', and about 'hypothetical' simple imperatives, can be extended in order to shed some light on the kindred and equally vexed problem of the so-called 'hypothetical' and 'categorical' uses of 'ought'. Without getting too much involved in the traditional terminology let us consider the following sentences, adapted by Prichard[1] from Kant:

(1) 'You ought to give a second dose' (said to a would-be poisoner).
(2) 'You ought to tell the truth.'

It is clear that the second sentence, on most occasions of its use, expresses a moral judgement, and equally clear that the

[1] *Moral Obligation*, p. 91.

first does not. It is not, however, equally clear that, as Prichard says and as Kant perhaps implies, we should conclude from this that there is 'a total difference of meaning' between the two uses of the word 'ought'; for in the sentences 'He is a good poisoner' and 'He is a good man', we can distinguish between the virtues (in the sense in which I have been using the term) requisite in a good poisoner, and those requisite in a good man, without necessarily distinguishing between two meanings of the word 'good', except in the secondary sense of 'meaning' in which to ask what 'good' means is just to ask for a list of the virtues. It may be that with 'ought', too, the word has the same meaning, in the primary sense, in the above two sentences, though in one case a moral judgement is expressed, and in the other not. For in the first sentence the context shows us that the standards which are being applied (the principles that are being referred to) are those for poisoning people; and in the second, we assume that the principles referred to are moral ones; but in each case the function of the word 'ought' is nothing but to refer to these principles and fulfil, in relation to them, the other functions outlined above. In the 'poisoner' case, to know that the principles referred to are those for poisoning is to know also something—but not everything—about what they are: they must at any rate enjoin the doing of such things as result in death by poison. Since 'poisoner' is a functional word in the sense defined above (6. 4), to know the class of comparison is to know something about the virtues; on the other hand with (2) this is not the case. But this does not constitute a difference between two meanings of the word 'ought'; it is a difference between two sets of principles. We have to tell from the context what set is being referred to; for since 'ought' is not an adjective like 'good', we do not have attached to it a noun (like 'poisoner' or 'man' in the sentences quoted) to tell us this. Therefore we may be mistaken in assuming that (2) is a moral judgement; it may only be intended as a prudential one. Even the judgement 'He is a good man' may not be a moral judgement; for 'man' may be an abbreviation for 'man to have with you in a fight' or 'man at a party' or 'man to put in to bat first'. In guessing which of these standards or sets of principles is being invoked, we are not at the same time guessing what 'good' or 'ought' means (except in the secondary sense); we know quite well what they mean.

All this does not mean that there is no important difference between moral principles and principles of successful poisoning. As we have seen (9. 2) we cannot get out of being men; and therefore moral principles, which are principles for the conduct of men as men—and not as poisoners or architects or batsmen—cannot be accepted without having a potential bearing upon the way that we conduct ourselves. If I say to a certain person 'You ought to tell the truth', I signify my acceptance of a principle to tell the truth in the sort of circumstances in which he is; and I may find myself placed unavoidably in similar circumstances. But I can always choose whether or not to take up poisoning or cricketing as a profession. This is bound to make the spirit in which we consider moral questions very different from that in which we consider how we ought to poison Jones, or build him a house; but the logic of the word 'ought' is not markedly different in the two cases.

It is true that in (2) above we can substitute for 'you ought', 'it is your duty', whereas in (1) we cannot. This is because the word 'duty' is restricted in respect of the classes of comparison within which it is used to commend; it is used almost exclusively for moral duties, legal duties, military duties, and other duties belonging to a particular station. Similarly the word 'brace', though its logic is the same as that of the word 'pair', is restricted largely to game-birds. But this does not affect what I have said.

'OUGHT' AND IMPERATIVES

11. 1. Since a large part of my argument hinges on the assumption, hitherto not fully defended, that value-judgements, if they are action-guiding, must be held to entail imperatives, and since this assumption may very well be questioned, it is time to examine it. It might be held, for example, that I can without contradiction say 'You ought to do A, but don't', and that therefore there can be no question of entailment; entailment in any case is a very strong word, and though many might be found to agree that value-judgements are action-guiding in some sense, it might be held that they are action-guiding only in the sense in which even plain judgements of fact may be action-guiding. For example, if I say 'The train is just about to depart', this may guide a person who wants to catch the train to take his seat; or, to take a moral case, if I say to a person who is thinking of giving some money to a friend supposedly in distress, 'The story he has just told you is quite untrue', this may guide him to make a different moral decision from that which he would otherwise have made. And similarly it might be held that value-judgements are action-guiding in no stronger sense than these statements of fact. It might be urged that, just as the statement that the train is going to depart has no bearing upon the practical problems of someone who does not want to catch the train, and just as, if the man who is thinking of giving money to his friend does not recognize that the truth or otherwise of his friend's story has any bearing on the question, it may not affect his decision, so, if a man has no intention of doing what he ought, to tell him that he ought to do something may not be accepted by him as a reason for doing it. I have put as forcibly as possible this objection, which strikes at the root of my whole argument. The objection alleges, in brief, that 'ought'-sentences are not imperatives, neither do they entail imperatives without the addition of an imperative premiss. In answer to this, I have to show that 'ought'-sentences, at any rate in some of their uses, do entail imperatives.

It is necessary first to recall something that I said earlier (7. 5) in discussing the evaluative and descriptive forces of value-judgements. We noticed that it is possible for people who have acquired very stable standards of values to come to treat value-judgements more and more as purely descriptive, and to let their evaluative force get weaker. The limit of this process is reached when, as we described it, the value-judgement 'gets into inverted commas', and the standard becomes completely 'ossified'. Thus it is possible to say 'You ought to go and call on the So-and-sos' meaning by it no value-judgement at all, but simply the descriptive judgement that such an action is required in order to conform to a standard which people in general, or a certain kind of people not specified but well understood, accept. And certainly, if this is the way in which an 'ought'-sentence is being used, it does not entail an imperative; we can certainly say without contradiction 'You ought to go and call on the So-and-sos, but don't'. I do not wish to claim that all 'ought'-sentences entail imperatives, but only that they do so when they are being used evaluatively. It will subsequently become apparent that I am making this true by definition; for I should not say that an 'ought'-sentence *was* being used evaluatively, unless imperatives were held to follow from it; but more of that later.

Thus one answer which we can make to the objection is that the cases which appear to support it are not genuine value-judgements. In the example quoted, if a man has no intention of doing what he ought, and if, therefore, telling him what he ought to do is not taken by him as entailing an imperative, that merely shows that, in so far as he accepts that he ought to do so-and-so (and of course *no* premiss enables a conclusion to be drawn unless it is accepted), he accepts it only in a non-evaluative, inverted-commas sense, as meaning that so-and-so falls within a class of actions which is generally held (but not by him) to be obligatory in the evaluative, imperative-entailing sense. This is an answer which disposes of some awkward cases, but which will not be accepted as a complete answer unless we extend its scope considerably. For it may be held that there are some genuine value-judgements which do not entail imperatives.

11. 2. Let us recall something else that I said earlier (4. 7). Practical principles, if they are accepted sufficiently long and unquestioningly, come to have the force of intuition. Thus our ultimate moral principles can become so completely accepted by us, that we treat them, not as universal imperatives, but as matters of fact; they have the same obstinate indubitability. And there is indeed a matter of fact to which it is very easy for us to take them as referring, namely, what we call our 'sense of obligation'. This is a concept that now requires investigation.

It is easy to see how, if we have been brought up from our earliest years in obedience to a principle, the thought of not obeying it becomes abhorrent to us. If we fail to obey it, we suffer remorse; when we do obey it, we feel at ease with ourselves. These feelings are reinforced by all those factors which psychologists have listed;[1] and the total result is what is generally called a feeling of obligation. It is a *fact* that we have this feeling of obligation—different people in different degrees, and with different contents. Judgements that I have a feeling of obligation to do X or Y are statements of empirical fact. This is not the place to argue about their interpretation; it is no doubt possible to dispute whether sentences like 'A is suffering from remorse' or 'B feels it is his duty to do Y' are reports of private mental events or are to be interpreted

---

[1] Cf. J. C. Flugel, *Man, Morals and Society*, especially ch. iii.

behaviouristically; but such controversies do not here concern us. Here it is important to point out a fact which has been singularly ignored by some moralists, that to say of someone that he has a feeling of obligation is not the same as to say that he has an obligation. To say the former is to make a statement of psychological fact; to say the latter is to make a value-judgement. A man who has been brought up in ar Army family, but has become affected by pacifism, may well say 'I have a strong feeling that I ought to fight for my country, but I wonder whether I really ought'. Similarly, a Japanese brought up in accordance with Bushido might say 'I have a strong feeling that I ought to torture this prisoner in order to extract information which will be to my Emperor's advantage; but ought I really to do so?'

The confusion between psychological statements about a feeling or sense of obligation and value-judgements about obligation itself is not confined to professional philosophers. The ordinary man so very rarely questions the principles in which he has been brought up, that he is usually willing, whenever he has a feeling that he ought to do X, to say on this ground alone that he ought to do X; and therefore he often gives voice to this feeling by saying 'I ought to do X'. This sentence is not a statement that he has the feeling; it is a value-judgement made as a result of having the feeling. For those, however, who have not studied the logical behaviour of value-judgements, and have not reflected on such examples as those of the pacifist and the Japanese just given, it is easy to take this remark as a statement of fact to the effect that he has the feeling, or to confuse it in meaning with this statement. But anyone, except a professional philosopher maintaining at all costs a moral sense theory, could be got to see that the meaning is not the same, by being asked 'Wouldn't it be possible for you to feel just like that, although you really oughtn't to do X?' or 'Mightn't you feel like that and be wrong?'

The confusion, however, goes deeper than this. We have
seen that there is a conscious inverted-commas use of value-
words in which, for example, 'I ought to do X' becomes
roughly equivalent to 'X is required in order to conform to a
standard which people in general accept'. But it is also
possible to use the word 'ought' and other value-words, as it
were, unconsciously in inverted commas; for the standard
which people in general accept may also be the standard
which one has been brought up to accept oneself, and therefore not only does one refer to this standard by saying 'I
ought to do X', but one has feelings of obligation to conform
to the standard.

It is then possible to treat 'I ought to do X' as a confused
mixture of three judgements.

(1) 'X is required in order to conform to the standard
which people generally accept' (statement of socio-
logical fact);
(2) 'I have a feeling that I ought to do X' (statement of
psychological fact);
(3) 'I ought to do X' (value-judgement).

Even this tripartite division conceals the complexity of the
meaning of such sentences; for each of the three elements is itself complex and can be taken in different senses. But even if we
confine ourselves to the three elements just given, it is usually
impossible for an ordinary person, untrained in logical subtle-
ties, to ask or to answer the question 'Which of these three
judgements are you making, just (1), or (1) and (2), or all
three, or some other combination?' The situation is very similar to that of the scientist who is asked by the logician 'Is
your statement that phosphorus melts at 44° C. analytic or
synthetic; if you found a substance which was in other respects just like phosphorus, but which melted at another
temperature, would you say "It isn't really phosphorus" or
would you say "Then after all some phosphorus melts at

other temperatures"?'[1] The scientist might well, as Mr. A. G. N. Flew has pointed out to me, answer 'I don't know; I haven't yet come across the case which would make me decide this question; I have got better things to worry about'. Similarly, the ordinary person, making moral decisions on the basis of his accepted principles, very rarely has to ask himself the question that we have just asked. So long as his value-judgements correspond with the accepted standards, and with his own feelings, he does not have to decide which he is saying, because, as we might put it, all three are as yet for him materially equivalent; that is to say, no occasion arises for saying one which is not also an occasion for saying the other two. He therefore does not ask himself 'As I am using the word "ought", are the sentences "I ought to do what I feel I ought" and "I ought to do what everybody would say I ought" analytic or synthetic?' It is the crucial case that makes him answer such a question; and in morals the crucial case comes when we are wondering whether to make a value-decision which is in disagreement with the accepted standards or with our own moral feelings—such cases as I have cited. It is these cases that really reveal the difference in meaning between the three judgements that I have listed.

My answer to the objection then is, that cases which are alleged to be value-judgements not entailing imperatives will always on examination be found to be cases where what is meant is not of type (3) above, but of type (1) or (2) or a mixture of both. This contention is, of course, impossible to prove or even to render plausible, unless we know when we are to count a judgement as of type (3); but I propose to get over this difficulty in the only possible way, by making it a matter of definition. I propose to say that the test, whether someone is using the judgement 'I ought to do X' as a value-judgement or not is, 'Does he or does he not recognize that if he assents to the judgement, he must also assent to the

[1] See G. H. von Wright, *Logical Problem of Induction*, ch. iii.

command "Let me do X"?' Thus I am not here claiming to prove anything substantial about the way in which we use language; I am merely suggesting a terminology which, if applied to the study of moral language, will, I am satisfied, prove illuminating. The substantial part of what I am trying to show is this, that, in the sense of 'value-judgement' just defined, we do make value-judgements, and that they are the class of sentences containing value-words which is of primary interest to the logician who studies moral language. Since what we are discussing is the logic of moral language and not that tangled subject known as moral psychology, I shall not here inquire farther into the fascinating problem, discussed by Aristotle, of *akrasia* or 'weakness of will'[1]—the problem presented by the person who thinks, or professes to think, that he ought to do something, but does not do it. The logical distinctions which I have been making shed considerable light on this question: but much more needs to be said, chiefly by way of a more thorough analysis of the phrase 'thinks that he ought'. For if we interpret my definition strictly, and take it in conjunction with what was said earlier (2. 2) about the criteria for 'sincerely assenting to a command', the familiar 'Socratic paradox' arises, in that it becomes analytic to say that everyone always[2] does what he thinks he ought to (in the evaluative sense). And this, to put Aristotle's objection in modern dress, is not how we use the word 'think'. The trouble arises because our criteria, in ordinary speech, for saying 'He thinks he ought' are exceedingly elastic. If a person does not do something, but the omission is accompanied by feelings of guilt, &c., we normally say that he has not done what he thinks he ought. It is therefore necessary to qualify the criterion given above for 'sincerely assenting to a command', and to admit that there are degrees of sincere assent, not all of which involve actually

[1] *Nicomachean Ethics*, VII. 1 ff.
[2] Strictly, 'always, if physically and psychologically able'; cf. p. 20.

obeying the command. But the detailed analysis of this problem requires much more space than I can give it here, and must wait for another occasion.

11. 3. The best way of establishing the primary logical interest of the evaluative sense of 'ought' is to show that, but for the existence of this sense, none of the familiar troubles generated by the word would arise. For of the three possible paraphrases of 'I ought to do X' given on p. 167, the first two are statements of fact. This is because, if they are expanded, it will be found that the word 'ought' in them always occurs in inverted commas or inside a subordinate clause beginning with 'that'. Thus (1) might be further paraphrased 'There is a principle of conduct which people generally accept, which says "One ought to do X in circumstances of a certain kind"; and I am now in circumstances of that kind'. Similarly, (2) might be further paraphrased 'The judgement "I ought to do X" evokes in me a feeling of conviction' or 'I find myself unable to doubt the judgement "I ought to do X"' (though the latter paraphrase is a good deal too strong; for not all feelings are irresistible; there is indeed an infinite gradation from vague uneasy stirrings of conscience to what are often called 'moral intuitions'). Now the fact, that when (1) and (2) are expanded the original judgement which they paraphrase occurs within them inside inverted commas, shows that there must be some sense of that original judgement which is not exhausted by (1) and (2); for if there were not, the sentence in the inverted commas would have in its turn to be paraphrased by (1) or (2), and we should be involved in an infinite regress. In the case of (1), I do not know any way of getting over this difficulty; in the case of (2), it can be got over temporarily by substituting for (2) some such paraphrase as 'I have a certain recognizable feeling'. But the device is only temporary; for if we are asked what this feeling is, or how we recognize it, the reply can only be 'It is the feeling called "a feeling of obligation"; it is the feeling you usually have when you say, and mean, "I ought to do so-and-so".'

This means that neither (1) nor (2) can give the primary sense of 'I ought to do X'. Now let us suppose (as is not the case) that (3) generates none of the logical puzzles of the kind that we have been discussing; let us suppose, that is to say, that (3) can be analysed naturalistically. If this were so, then these puzzles would not arise in the cases of (1) or (2) either; for since, besides the expression in inverted commas, there is nothing else in the expansions of (1) and (2) that cannot be analysed naturalistically, it would be possible to effect a completely naturalistic analysis of all uses of 'ought', and thus of 'good' (12. 3). The fact that this is not possible is entirely due to the intractably evaluative character of (3). It is due ultimately to the impossibility, mentioned earlier (2. 5) of deriving imperatives from indicatives; for (3), by definition, entails at least one imperative; but if (3) were analysable naturalistically, this would mean that it was equivalent to a series of indicative sentences; and this would constitute a breach of the principle established. Thus it is this fact, that in some of its uses 'ought' is used evaluatively (i.e. as entailing at least one imperative) that makes a naturalistic analysis impossible, and hence generates all the difficulties that we have been considering. A logician who neglects these uses will make his task easy, at the cost of missing the essential purpose of moral language.

It is this, above all, that makes the first part of this book relevant to what is discussed in the remainder. For all the words discussed in Parts II and III have it as their distinctive function either to commend or in some other way to guide choices or actions; and it is this essential feature which defies any analysis in purely factual terms. But to guide choices or actions, a moral judgement has to be such that if a person assents to it, he must assent to some imperative sentence derivable from it; in other words, if a person does not assent to some such imperative sentence, that is knock-down evidence that he does not assent to the moral judgement in an evaluative sense—though of course he may assent to it in some other sense (e.g. one of those I have mentioned). This is true by my definition of the word 'evaluative'. But to say this is to say that if he professes to assent to the moral judgement, but does not assent to the imperative, he must have misunderstood the moral judgement (by taking it to be non-evaluative, though the speaker intended it to be evaluative). We are therefore clearly entitled to say that the moral judgement entails the imperative; for to say that one judgement entails another is simply to say that you cannot assent to the first and dissent from the second unless you have misunderstood one or the other; and this 'cannot' is a logical 'cannot'—if someone assents to the first and not to the second, this is in itself a sufficient criterion for saying that he has misunderstood the meaning of one or the other. Thus to say that moral judgements guide actions, and to say that they entail imperatives, comes to much the same thing.

I do not in the least wish to deny that moral judgements are sometimes used non-evaluatively, in my sense. All I wish to assert is that they are sometimes used evaluatively, and that it is this use which gives them the special characteristics to which I have drawn attention; and that, if it were not for this use, it would be impossible to give a meaning to the other uses; and also that, if it were not for the logical difficulties connected with the evaluative use, the other uses could be analysed naturalistically. Ethics, as a special branch of logic, owes its existence to the function of moral judgements as a guide in answering questions of the form 'What shall I do?'

11. 4. I am now in a position to answer an objection which may have occurred to some readers. Writers on ethics often condemn 'naturalism' or some related fallacy in others, only to commit it themselves in a subtler form. It may be alleged

that I have done this. I suggested earlier (5. 3) that the term
'naturalist' should be reserved for such ethical theories as are
open to refutation on lines similar to those marked out by
Professor Moore. We must therefore ask whether any analogous refutation of my own theory can be constructed. Now
it is true that I am not suggesting that moral judgements can
be deduced from any statements of fact. In particular I am
not suggesting the adoption of definitions of value-terms of
the sort which Moore mistakenly attributed to Kant. Moore
accused Kant of saying that 'This ought to be' means 'This
is commanded'.[1] This definition would be naturalistic; for
'A is commanded' is a statement of fact; it is expansible into
'Someone [it is not disclosed who] has said "Do A"'. The
fact that the imperative is in inverted commas prevents it
affecting the mood of the complete sentence. Needless to say,
I am not suggesting any such equivalence, either for 'good'
or for 'ought' or for any other value-word, except perhaps
when they are used in what I have called an 'inverted-
commas' sense, or in some other purely descriptive way. But
it might nevertheless be said that according to my treatment
of moral judgements certain sentences would become analytic
which in ordinary usage are not analytic—and this would be
very like Moore's refutation. For example, consider sentences
like the Psalmist's

Eschew evil and do good,[2]

or the line of John Wesley's hymn

In duty's path go on.[3]

On my theory these would, it might be alleged, become analytic; for from 'A is evil' is deducible the imperative sentence
'Eschew A', and from 'Path P is the path of duty' is deducible
the imperative sentence 'Go on in path P'.

[1] *Principia Ethica*, pp. 127–8.   [2] Ps. xxxiv, v. 14.
[3] *Hymns Ancient and Modern* (1950), no. 310.

Now it must be noticed that such sentences as those quoted are expansible into sentences in which a value-judgement occurs in a subordinate clause. Thus if, instead of the archaic 'Eschew evil' we write 'Do not do what is evil', this can be expanded into 'For all X, if X is evil, do not do X'. For this instruction to be applied, it is necessary that we should conjoin it with a minor premiss 'A is evil', and from the two premisses conclude 'Do not do A'. For this reasoning to be helpful, it is necessary that the minor premiss 'A is evil' should be a statement of fact; there must be a criterion for telling unambiguously whether it is true or false. This means that in this premiss the word 'evil' must have a descriptive meaning (whatever further meaning it may have). But if the reasoning is to be valid, the word 'evil' in the major premiss must have the same meaning as in the minor; there also, therefore, it must have a descriptive meaning. Now it is this descriptive content which prevents the major premiss being analytic. Sentences of the sort we are discussing are normally used by people who have firmly established value-standards, and whose value-words have, therefore, a large element of descriptive meaning. In the sentence 'Do not do what is evil', the evaluative content of 'evil' is for the moment neglected; the speaker, as it were, lets his support of the standard slip for a moment, only in order to ram it back into place with the imperative verb. This is a first-class exercise in the maintenance of our standards, and that is why it is so much in place in hymns and psalms. But it can only be performed by those who are in no doubt as to what the standard is.

Contrast with these cases others which are superficially similar. Suppose that I am asked 'What shall I do?', and answer 'Do whatever is best' or 'Do what you ought to do'. In most contexts such answers would be regarded as unhelpful. It would be as if a policeman were asked 'Where shall I park my car?' and replied 'Wherever it is legitimate to park it'. I am asked by the speaker to give definite advice as to what he is to do; he asks me, just because he does not know what standard to apply in his case. If, therefore, I reply by telling him to conform to some standard as to whose provisions he is quite in the dark, I do not give him any useful advice. Thus in such a context the sentence 'Do whatever is best' really *is* analytic; for because the standard is assumed to be unknown, 'best' has no descriptive meaning.

Thus my account of the meaning of value-words is not naturalistic; it does not result in sentences becoming analytic which are not so in our ordinary usage. Rather it shows, by doing full justice to both the descriptive and the evaluative elements in the meaning of value-words, how it is that they play in our ordinary usage the role that they do play. A somewhat similar difficulty is presented by Satan's famous paradox 'Evil be thou my good'. This yields to the same type of analysis, but for reasons of space I am compelled to leave the reader to unravel the problem himself.

11. 5. It may be asked at this point 'Are you not assimilating moral judgements too much to the ordinary universal imperatives that exist in most languages?' It has indeed been objected to all imperative analyses of moral judgements, that they would make a moral judgement like 'You ought not to smoke (in this compartment)' the equivalent of the universal imperative 'No Smoking'. And they are clearly not equivalent, though both, according to the theory which I have been advocating, entail 'Do not smoke'. It is therefore necessary to state what it is that distinguishes 'You ought not to smoke' from 'No smoking'. I have already touched on this problem, but it requires further discussion.

The first thing to notice about 'No smoking' is that it is not a proper universal, because it implicitly refers to an individual; it is short for 'Do not ever smoke in *this* compartment'. The moral judgement 'You ought not to smoke in this compartment' also contains references to individuals; for the pronouns 'you' and 'this' occur in it. But, in view of what I have said above (10. 3), this is not the end of the matter. The moral judgement 'You ought not to smoke in this compartment' has to be made with some general moral principle in mind, and its purpose must be either to invoke that general principle or to point to an instance of its application. The principle might be 'One ought never to smoke in compartments in which there are young children' or 'One ought never to smoke in compartments in which there is a "No Smoking" notice'. It is not always easy to elicit just what the principle is; but it always makes sense to ask what it is. The speaker cannot deny that there is any such principle. The same point might be put another way by saying that if we make a particular moral judgement, we can always be asked to support it by reasons; the reasons consist in the general principles under which the moral judgement is to be subsumed. Thus the particular moral judgement 'You ought not to smoke in this compartment' depends on a proper universal, even though it is not itself one. But this is not true of the imperative 'Do not ever smoke in this compartment'. This invokes no more general principle; it is itself as general as it requires to be, and this is not general enough to make it a proper universal.

The difference in universality between 'Do not ever smoke in this compartment' and 'You ought not to smoke in this compartment' may be brought out in the following way. Suppose that I say to someone 'You ought not to smoke in this compartment', and there are children in the compartment. The person addressed is likely, if he wonders why I have said that he ought not to smoke, to look around, notice the children, and so understand the reason. But suppose that, having ascertained everything that is to be ascertained about the compartment, he then says 'All right; I'll go next door; there's another compartment there just as good; in fact it is exactly like this one, and there are children in it too'. I should think if he said this that he did not understand the function of the word 'ought'; for 'ought' always refers to some general principle; and if the next compartment is really exactly like this one, every principle that is applicable to this one must be applicable to the other (8. 2). I might therefore reply 'But look here, if you oughtn't to smoke in this compartment, and the other compartment is just like this one, has the same sort of occupants, the same notices on the windows, &c., then obviously you oughtn't to smoke in that one either'. On the other hand, when the Railway Executive is making the momentous decision, on which compartments to put notices saying 'No Smoking', nobody says 'Look here! You've put a notice on this compartment, so you must put one on the one next to it, because it's exactly like it'. This is because 'No Smoking' does not refer to a universal principle of which this compartment is an instance.

It is, in fact, almost impossible to frame a proper universal in the imperative mood. Suppose that we try to do this by generalizing the sentence 'Do not ever smoke in this compartment'. First we eliminate the implicit 'you' by writing 'No one is ever to smoke in this compartment'. We then have to eliminate the 'this'. A step towards this is taken by writing 'No one is ever to smoke in any compartment of British Railways'. But we still have left here the proper name 'British Railways'. We can only achieve a proper universal by excluding all proper names, for example by writing 'No one is ever to smoke in any railway compartment anywhere'. This is a proper universal; but it is a sentence which no one could ever have occasion to utter. Commands are always addressed to someone or to some individual set (not class) of people. It is not clear what could be meant by the sentence just quoted, unless it were a *moral* injunction or other value-judgement. Suppose that we imagine God issuing such a command. Then it becomes at once like the Ten Commandments in form. Historically speaking 'Honour thy father and thy mother' is supposed to have been said, not to everyone in general, but only to members of the chosen people, just as 'Render to no man evil for evil' was addressed to Christ's disciples, not to the world at large—though He intended that all men should become His disciples. But suppose that this were not so; suppose that 'Render to no man evil for evil' were addressed literally to the unlimited class 'every man'. Should we not say that it had become equivalent in meaning to the value-judgement 'One ought to render to no man evil for evil'? Similarly, a proverbial expression like 'Let sleeping dogs lie' may without much of a jolt be paraphrased by the (prudential) value-judgement 'One ought to let sleeping dogs lie'.

On the other hand, ordinary so-called universal imperatives like 'No Smoking' are distinguished from value-judgements by not being properly universal. We are thus able to discriminate between these two kinds of sentence, without in the least abandoning anything that I have said about the relation between value-judgements and imperatives. For both the complete universal and the incomplete entail the singular: 'Do not ever smoke in this compartment' entails 'Do not (now) smoke in this compartment'; and so does 'You ought not to smoke in this compartment', if it is used evaluatively. But the latter also entails, as the former does not, 'No one ought to smoke in any compartment exactly like this one', and this in its turn entails 'Do not smoke in any compartment exactly like this one'.

These considerations alone, however, would not be sufficient to account altogether for the complete difference in 'feel' between 'You ought not' and 'Do not ever'. This is reinforced by two other factors. The first has already been alluded to; the complete universality of the moral judgement means that we cannot 'get away from it'; and therefore its acceptance is a much more serious matter than the acceptance of an imperative from whose range of application we can escape. This would explain why imperatives such as those laws of a State, which are of very general application, and therefore very difficult to escape from, have a 'feel' much more akin to moral judgements than have the regulations of the Railway Executive. But a more important additional factor is that, partly because of their complete universality, moral principles have become so entrenched in our minds—in the ways already described—that they have acquired a quasi-factual character, and are indeed sometimes used non-evaluatively as statements of fact and nothing else, as we have seen. None of this is true of imperatives like 'No Smoking'; and this in itself would be quite enough to explain the difference in 'feel' between the two kinds of sentence. Since, however, I do not wish to deny that there are non-evaluative uses of moral judgements, but only to assert that there are evaluative uses, this difference in 'feel' in no way destroys my argument. It would indeed be absurd to pretend that 'No Smoking' is in all respects like 'You ought not to smoke'; I have been maintaining only that it is like it in one respect, that both entail singular imperatives such as 'Do not smoke (now)'.

12

AN ANALYTICAL MODEL

12. 1. It may help to clarify the relations between the language of values and the imperative mood if we now carry out the following experiment: let us imagine that our language does not contain any value-words; and let us then ask, to what extent a new artificial terminology, defined in terms of the imperative mood and of the ordinary logical words, could fill the gap which this would leave. In other words, could we, using only the imperative mood and words defined in terms of it, do all or any of the jobs that are done in ordinary language by means of value-words like 'good', 'right', and 'ought'? In order to make as clear as possible the parallel between our new artificial language and ordinary value-language, I shall use the same words in both, but shall print the artificial ones in italics. I wish to make it quite clear that I am not suggesting a definitive analysis of the value-words of ordinary language. They are indeed so varied in their uses and so subtly flexible that any artificial construction is bound to be a travesty of them. Nor am I committing the sin of 'reductionism' which, because of its excessive prevalence, has become a fashionable target for philosophical heresy-hunters. I am not, that is to say, trying to analyse one kind of language in terms of another; I am trying, rather, to exhibit the differences and similarities between two kinds of language, by seeing what modifications would have to be made to one, before it could do the job of the other, and how adequately, so modified, it could do it.

My procedure will be as follows: I shall first simplify the problem by showing that, if we can do the job of 'ought', we can also do the job of 'right' and 'good'; for I shall show that (in the rough and ready way which is all that such methods ever offer), sentences compounded with 'ought' can take the place of sentences containing the other two words. I shall then tackle the word 'ought'. To this end I shall inquire what has to be done to the ordinary imperative mood in order to make it a suitable instrument for our purpose. I shall show how the imperative mood might be modified in such a way as to make it possible to frame in it proper universal sentences. I shall then, in terms of this modified imperative mood, define a concept '*ought*', which will serve as the simplest and most basic of my artificial value-words. If this were intended as an analysis of the words 'ought', 'right', and 'good' as they occur in ordinary language, the procedure would indeed be foolhardy; but my italics will serve as a recurrent warning to the reader that this is not what I am attempting. I have already said in the preceding chapters all that I have room to say about the logical behaviour of these words in ordinary language; my present purpose is quite different, and much more tentative.

12. 2. First, then, we must see to what extent an artificial word '*right*', defined in terms of the ordinary word 'ought', could take the place of 'right' in ordinary language. I shall not consider all the uses of 'right', but shall confine myself to those which seem to be the most important. The first is where we say 'It is not (or in a particular case would not be or was not) right to do so-and-so'. There are both moral and non-moral judgements of this form; thus we may say 'It was not right to joke about Jones so soon after his death, with his widow present' or 'It was not right to put in Smith to bat first when he had just finished a long spell of bowling'. This use is always in the negative; there is, however, a parallel use in the affirmative, as: 'It was quite right to change the subject' and 'It was right to give Smith a rest'. Again, there is the use in which 'right' is always preceded by the definite article, and is not predicative but goes with a noun; here, too, there are both moral and non-moral examples; we may say 'The right thing to do would have been to change the subject' or 'Robinson was the right man for the job'.

Now if, as we are going to assume, our language did not contain the word 'right', but did contain the word 'ought', we might make shift by defining in terms of 'ought' an artificial word '*right*' to do the job now done by 'right'. We should have to have different definitions for the different uses; and if I were being very exact, I should have to distinguish these uses by different subscripts, writing '*right*$_1$', '*right*$_2$', &c. This, however, is hardly necessary in a sketch of this character. The definitions which I propose are as follows. 'It is not *right* to do A' is to mean the same as 'One ought not to do A'. 'It would not be *right* for X to do A' is to mean the same as 'X ought not to do A'. 'It was not *right* for X to do A' is to mean the same as 'X ought not to have done A'. 'It would not have been *right* for X to do A' is to mean the same as 'If X had done A, he would have done what he ought not'. These examples are sufficient to give an idea of how we should deal with the first use of 'right'.

The second use is treated similarly. 'It was *right* for X to do A' is to mean the same as 'X, in doing A, did what he ought'. Note that there is a different use of 'right', not among those considered above, in which it has almost the meaning 'all right'. 'It was all right for X to do A' cannot be rendered in the way just suggested; we should have to say that 'It was *all right* for X to do A' is to mean the same as 'In doing A, X did not do what he ought not'.

The third use requires a slightly different treatment. 'The *right* A' is to mean 'The A which ought to be (or ought to have been) chosen'. Thus 'He is (or would have been) the *right* man for the job' is to mean the same as 'He is the man who ought to be (or ought to have been) chosen for the job', and 'The *right* thing to have done would have been to change the subject' is to mean the same as 'He ought to have changed the subject'. Note that there is a complication here which I shall ignore, since it has nothing to do with ethics: the expression 'He ought to have done A' usually either implies that he did not do A, or else is inapposite unless in fact he did not do A. A full formal analysis would require an extra clause to deal with this peculiarity; but it need not here detain us.

Sometimes the word 'chosen' requires supplementation in order to bring out the full meaning, by giving the class of comparison. Thus, in order to render in our artificial terminology 'He did not call at the right house' we shall have to say that 'He did not call at the *right* house' is to mean the same as 'He did not call at the house which he ought to have chosen to call at' and not, for example, 'He did not call at the house which he ought to have chosen to blow up with dynamite'. It may be safely predicted that, if we had to make shift with my artificial word '*right*', we should not find it difficult to supply a speaker's meaning from the context, just as we do with the natural word 'right'.

I shall not examine in detail, to what extent '*right*' would be an adequate substitute for 'right'. My impression is that we could get along with it quite well. It would be absurd, however, to claim that any artificial word could ever do exactly all the jobs, and no others, that are done by a natural word; our ordinary language is much too subtle, flexible, and complicated to be imitated in this offhand way.

12. 3. Let us now follow the same procedure with 'good'. The definition of our artificial word '*good*' is a great deal more complicated than that of '*right*' for the following reason: as has been noticed by more than one writer on ethics, the comparative 'better than' is much easier to define than the positive. In this 'good' is like 'hot'. We can give quite simple and adequate criteria for deciding whether object X is hotter than object Y; but if we are asked to give exact criteria for saying whether an object is hot, we shall be quite unable to do so. All we can do is to explain the meaning of 'hotter than', and then to say that an object is said to be hot, if it is hotter than usual for an object of its class. The last half of this explanation is extremely loose; and logicians would be wise to leave it so, for 'hot' is a loose word. 'Good' is a loose word for the same reason—and it is important to notice that, as the parallel with 'hot' shows, this looseness has nothing to do with the fact that 'good' is a value-word. There are, indeed, other features of 'good', originating in its character as a value-word, which have also earned for it the name 'loose'— e.g. the fact that its descriptive meaning can vary according to the standard that is being applied. That, however, has nothing to do with the present problem; for in the latter sense 'better than' is as loose (if that is the right word) as 'good'; but the kind of looseness to which I am now referring attaches only to the positive and not to the comparative.

Let us then try to define an artificial concept '*better* than' in terms of 'ought'. The following definition may be suggested: 'A is a *better* X than B' is to mean the same as 'If one is choosing an X, then, if one chooses B, one ought to choose A'. Since this definition is complicated, the point of it may at first be missed. We must remember, first of all, that a conditional sentence is false only when the antecedent is true and the consequent false. This may be said, whatever view we take as to the possibility of defining 'if' truth-functionally. Now suppose, for example, that I am asked by a pupil to advise him on the respective merits of several courses of lectures on Aristotle's *Ethics*. I might say 'A's lectures on the *Ethics* are *better* (for your purposes) than B's'. Now we have to ask: Under what conditions should I say that my pupil had not taken my advice? Suppose that we assume that he always does what he thinks he ought to do. Then if he goes to A's lectures and not to B's, he is following my advice. Even if he goes to both, I shall not be able to accuse him of disregarding my advice; for he may still think that A's are *better* than B's. The same is true if he goes to neither. In one case only can I accuse him of not taking my advice: this is if he goes to B's but not to A's; for this shows that, in a case when he is choosing between lectures on the *Ethics*, and has chosen to go to B's, he does not think that he ought also to go to A's; and he would have to think this, according to my definition, if he thought that A's were *better* than B's.

Now I think that it will be agreed that '*better* than', as so defined, could do fairly adequately the job that is done in ordinary language by 'better than'. But in the case of moral uses there is a complication that has occupied the attention of many writers on ethics and is one of the bases of the much-emphasized distinction between the words 'right' and 'good' as used in morals.[1] It is a commonplace that to say that a certain act was right is not to say that it was a good act; for to be good it has to be done from a good motive, whereas to be right it has merely to conform to a certain principle, from whatever motive it is done. Thus, if I pay my tailor's bill in the hope that he will spend it on excessive drinking, I still do right to pay him, though it is not a good act, because my motive is bad. It may also be said, that to say that a person did something that was not right (not what he ought to have done) is not necessarily to condemn or blame him for it; for although he did what was not right, he may have acted from the best of motives, or may not have been able to resist a temptation which he could not be blamed for failing to resist. It is possible, in terms of my definition of '*better* than' and thus of '*good*', to make this distinction much clearer than it has hitherto been. We have to modify the definition slightly; for in terms of it, 'A was a *better* act in the circumstances than B' would simply mean 'If one is choosing what act to do in circumstances like that, then, if one chooses B, one ought to choose A'. Thus if the definition were applied directly it would not contain the necessary reference to the motives from which the act was done. It is therefore necessary to proceed indirectly, and, adapting Aristotle's remark, to say that a *good*

[1] See Sir David Ross, *The Right and the Good*, pp. 4 ff.

act is the sort of act that a *good* man would do.[1] Then, in terms of our definition, we define a *good* man as follows: he is a man who is *better* than men usually are; and to say that A is a *better* man than B is to say that if one is choosing what sort of man to be, then, if one chooses to be the sort of man that B is, one ought to choose to be the sort of man that A is; and since, *ex hypothesi*, A is not the same sort of man as B is, this boils down to saying that if we choose to be like either A or B, it ought to be A that we choose to be like.

This somewhat complicated definition of '*good* act' may be explained more simply and roughly as follows: when we are speaking of a good act we are speaking of the act as indicative of the goodness of the man; and when we speak of the goodness of a man, the choices that we are seeking to guide are not primarily those of people who are in just that sort of situation in which he did the act (e.g. the situation of receiving a bill from one's tailor) but those of people who are asking themselves 'What sort of man ought I to try to become?' We talk about good men and good acts in a context of moral education and character-formation, whereas we talk of right acts in a different context, that in which we are speaking of duties on particular sorts of occasion which can be fulfilled whether the character or set of motives of the agent is good or bad. If this is indeed how we use 'good act', then the word '*good*', as I have treated it, brings out very well this feature of the natural word 'good'.

The whole of my analysis so far has been very rough and ready, and even so it has been extremely complicated and difficult to follow. If I had made it more exact, it would have been still more difficult; and I do not know any way of making it easier. I can only hope that I have been able to give the reader a sufficient idea of the sort of way in which we could, if 'good' and 'right' dropped out of our language, supply the deficiency by using the word 'ought'. My im-

---

[1] *Nicomachean Ethics*, 1143^{b}23.

pression is that, though the new artificial words would at first appear clumsy compared with the old, we should be able to make shift with them when we required to say what we now say by means of the natural words 'good' and 'right'.

12. 4. We have so far been using in our definitions the natural word 'ought'. We have now to inquire whether, if this in turn were denied to us, we could make do with an artificial concept '*ought*', defined in terms of an enriched imperative mood. This is the part of my analysis which is likely to excite the most scepticism. We have first to show what we have to do to the imperative mood, in order to be able to frame in it proper universal sentences; and then in terms of these proper universal imperatives to define '*ought*' in such a way that it can perform the various functions of 'ought'.

The reasons why proper universal sentences cannot be framed in the imperative mood are two. In the first place this mood is confined, with a few exceptions which are apparent only, to the future tense, whereas a proper universal sentence has to apply to all times, past, present, and future (e.g. 'All mules are barren' has to apply to all mules at all periods of the world's history if it is to be a proper universal; we have to be able to derive from it, in conjunction with 'Joe was a mule', the sentence 'Joe was barren'). Secondly, the imperative mood occurs predominantly in the second person; there are some first person plural imperatives, and some third person imperatives in singular and plural; there is also a form 'Let me . . .' which serves as a first person singular imperative. But these persons are of different form, in English, from the second person, and may be of a somewhat different logical character. More serious is the difficulty that there is no means of framing an imperative sentence beginning with 'one' or with the impersonal 'you': there is nothing in the imperative mood analogous to the indicative sentence 'One does not see many hansom cabs nowadays' or the value-judgement 'One ought not to tell lies'. It is obvious that, if we are to be able to frame proper universal imperatives, they must be such that, with the aid of the appropriate minor premisses, we can derive from them imperative sentences in all the per· sons, as well as in all the tenses. The imperative mood, therefore, has for our purposes to be enriched in order to make it possible to frame sentences in all persons and all tenses.

The notion of so enriching the mood, by producing sentences (such as past imperatives) that could have no use in our language, may well excite suspicion. It is obvious why we never command things to happen in the past; and therefore it might be said that a past imperative would be meaningless. I am not concerned to deny this—for in a sense an expression *is* meaningless if it could have no possible use; but nevertheless it will be seen that these sentences do have a function in my analysis, and therefore I must ask the reader to put up with them. There is perhaps an analogy with the use of imaginary numbers in mathematics. It is at this point that the essential difference between the imperatives of ordinary language and value-judgements is most clearly revealed; since, however, my analysis is intended to expose distinctions, not to conceal them, this constitutes no defect in it.

12. 5. In order to enrich the imperative mood with regard to tense and person, I shall use a device derived from my previous discussion of the constitution of imperative sentences in 2. 1. There we saw that an imperative sentence, like an indicative one, consists of two elements, which I called the phrastic and the neustic. The phrastic is that part of the sentence which is common to the indicative and imperative moods; thus the sentences 'You are about to shut the door' and 'Shut the door' can be analysed in such a way as to have the same phrastic; they would then be written respectively

Shutting of the door by you in the immediate future, yes.

and

Shutting of the door by you in the immediate future, please.

The neustic is that part of the sentence which determines its mood. It is represented by 'yes' (indicative) and 'please' (imperative) in the two sentences just quoted. Now the tense-indication of a sentence goes into the phrastic. But since there are indicative sentences in all tenses, there must be phrastics in all tenses; and it is therefore possible to take the phrastic of an indicative sentence, add to it the imperative neustic, and we shall then have a past imperative sentence. Thus we might write

Shutting of the door by you last night, please.

We could also have tenseless imperatives, by making use of a time-scale instead of tenses; thus we might write

Shutting of the door by you at 11 p.m. on 4 March, please.

Thus, provided that the initial aversion to past imperatives is overcome, there is no logical difficulty in forming them. The same is true of the other tenses.

A similar device enables us to construct imperative sentences in any person. All we have to do is to take the phrastic of an indicative sentence in that person, and put after it the imperative neustic. Alternatively, we may forgo personal pronouns altogether, and substitute either proper names or definite or indefinite descriptions. Finally, we may, as we require to do, take the phrastic of a proper universal indicative sentence and, by putting an imperative neustic after it, get a proper universal imperative sentence. Thus we may take the indicative sentence 'All mules are barren' and write it thus:

All mules being barren, yes.

The proper universal imperative sentence will then be written:

All mules being barren, please.

This differs in meaning from the imperative of ordinary language 'Let all mules be barren' in that the latter can refer only to future mules, whereas the former is a fiat directed to all mules, past and present as well as future. Thus, if a mule in 23 B.C. produced offspring, this would not be a breach of the command 'Let all mules be barren' said in A.D. 1952, but it would be a breach of a proper universal command uttered at any time; and this is important for our purpose, for actions can be breaches of 'ought'-principles that have not yet been uttered; that is the point of the expression 'ought to have'.

Now if we frame suitable proper universal sentences in this enriched imperative mood, we shall see that they approach in meaning to value-judgements. We have already considered the universal imperative of ordinary language 'Render to no man evil for evil', and seen that, if it were considered as a proper universal, it would be roughly equivalent in meaning to 'One ought to render to no man evil for evil'. As it occurs in the Gospel, it cannot be so taken, because it is addressed to a definite collection of people, Christ's disciples, and does not apply to anyone who is not a disciple; and the same is generally true of imperative sentences; they have, as we have seen, a restricted application. Moreover 'Render to no man evil for evil' is undeniably future in its application. If someone had, at the moment it was uttered, just finished revenging himself upon an enemy, he would not have been disobeying the command. But in our modified imperative mood we can frame a principle of complete universality, such that an action at any time whatever, done by any person whatever, could have been a breach of it. And this is what a moral principle or other 'ought'-principle is like.

Instead, therefore, of the cumbrous terminology of phrastics and neustics, let us adopt the artificial word *'ought'*. This is to be defined as follows: if we take a proper universal indicative sentence 'All P's are Q' and split it into phrastic and neustic, 'All P's being Q, yes', and then substitute for the indicative neustic an imperative one 'All P's being Q, please', we may, instead of the latter sentence, write 'All P's *ought* to be Q'.

So far, this definition only gives the meaning of '*ought*' as it might be used to frame sentences fulfilling the function of the general 'ought'-principles or type B sentences referred to in 10. 3. That is to say, it offers a substitute for sentences like 'If the engine fails to start at once on the self-starter, one ought always to use the starting-handle', or 'One ought always to speak the truth'. These have only to be recast, in order to fall within the universal formula: 'All attempts to start the engines of motor vehicles which have failed to start at once on the self-starter ought to consist in using the starting-handle', and 'All things that are said ought to be true'. If '*ought*' were a proper substitute for 'ought', sentences of this type would be provided for by my definition. On the other hand, sentences of types C and D, which are singular 'ought'-sentences, future and past, are not so far catered for. Their analysis is an extremely complex matter, but we may suggest the following substitute: instead of 'You ought to tell him the truth', let us write 'If you do not tell him the truth, you will be breaking a general "*ought*"-principle to which I hereby subscribe'. And similarly, instead of 'You ought to have told him the truth', let us write 'In not telling him the truth, you broke a general "*ought*"-principle to which I hereby subscribe'. More formally, we might write 'There is at least one value for P and one for Q such that (1) all P's *ought* to be Q and (2) your not telling him the truth would be (or was) a case of a P not being Q'. Here again, if '*ought*' is a proper substitute for 'ought', sentences of types C and D would be covered by my definition.

In making this comparison it is to be noticed first of all that '*ought*', as I have defined it, has one important characteristic which the natural word 'ought' also has, and which distinguishes them both from simple imperatives. This

characteristic is due to the fact that the sentences in which
'*ought*' and 'ought' occur are always (or at least always depend
on) proper universals. It has sometimes been maintained that
the logic of 'ought'-sentences is in some sense three-valued
(that is to say, that the law of the excluded middle does not apply to them); if I deny that X ought to do A, it does not follow
that I am logically bound to affirm that X ought not to do A.
It may be that, as we say, it does not matter whether X does
A or not, and therefore it may be impossible to affirm, either
that he ought to do A, or that he ought not to do A. Now all
universal sentences have this character, as was recognized,
long before three-valued logics were thought of, in the traditional Aristotelian logic. 'All P's are Q' and 'All P's are not-
Q' (or 'No P's are Q') are not contradictories but contraries;
and therefore if we deny that all P's are Q, we do not thereby
compel ourselves to affirm that no P's are Q; for some
P's may be Q and some not. It is not necessary here to
discuss whether to speak of a three-valued logic is the
best way of describing this characteristic of universal sentences; but the similarity, in this respect, between 'ought'-
sentences and universal sentences lends support to my
definition.

12. 6. We have now to ask, whether '*ought*' is a complete
substitute for 'ought'—whether with its aid we can do all the
jobs which in ordinary language we do with the latter word.
Now these jobs may be divided into two classes: first, those
which are properly evaluative or prescriptive, and, secondly,
those which are descriptive. Of these, it will be found that the
former are adequately provided for by '*ought*', whereas the
latter are not without further definition, and then not so
handily. We saw above that the evaluative uses of 'ought'
were those which entailed singular imperatives. It is clear
that '*ought*', as I have defined it, fulfils this function. This
means that it can be used for all those functions of 'ought'
which consist in moral or any other kind of teaching or

advice. Thus, if we use '*ought*'-sentences in teaching someone
to drive, he will be instructed as clearly and efficiently as if
we used the 'ought'-sentences of ordinary language. When he
has been taught by this means, he will know, on all kinds of
occasion which have been covered by our instructions, just what
to do. And the same is true of moral teaching, whether it is of
the sort given by fathers to their children or whether of the
sort given by great moral innovators like the Buddha or Christ.
The fact that both the former and the latter class of teachers
often, as it is, use imperatives and not 'ought'-sentences lends
support to what I have said. We have already considered
'Render to no man evil for evil'; and fathers often say things
like 'If you must fight, fight someone your own size, not your
baby sister'. The intention of such a remark is clearly moral.

On the other hand, '*ought*', as I have defined it, would not
so adequately perform the descriptive functions which the
word 'ought' has in ordinary language. Let us consider an
example from a previous chapter. Suppose that I say 'At the
very moment when he ought to have been arriving at the play,
he was grovelling underneath his car five miles away'. As we
have seen, this is not primarily a way of telling people at
what time one ought to turn up at plays; it is a way of giving
them information about what the man referred to was doing
at a certain time; what this time is will be at once apparent
to anyone who knows at what time one ought to turn up at
plays; and this they know, because everyone agrees that one
ought (evaluative) to turn up at plays shortly before they begin.
Thus because everyone agrees in a particular evaluation,
there grows up a secondary use of 'ought' in which it can be
used to give information. Now this secondary use is not
catered for by '*ought*' as I have defined it so far. It is true
that, in cases where, as here, it is not unnatural to treat the
imperative contained in '*ought*' as a hypothetical one, the
considerations advanced in 3.2 may help us out; for hypothetical imperatives are in some sense descriptive, the major

premiss being supplied or understood. But this will not cover all cases. A way out of the problem is offered, however, if we make use of the 'inverted-commas' technique already referred to (7. 5). We might rewrite the sentence 'At the very moment when most people (myself included) would agree in saying "He *ought* to have been arriving at the play", he was, &c.' This is on the surface an indicative sentence, because the '*ought*' which entails the imperative is inside inverted commas; the imperative is not used but only mentioned.

It is interesting to notice the difference between this expression 'most people (myself included) would agree' and the expression used in a previous and fully evaluative example 'to which I hereby subscribe' (12. 4). If I say 'I hereby subscribe to such and such a principle', that is as good as actually enunciating the principle; the words 'hereby subscribe', as it were, cancel out the inverted commas, in the same way as 'I hereby promise that I will obey, serve, love, &c.' would have the same force in the marriage service as 'I will obey, serve, love, &c.' Thus in the sentence 'If you do not tell him the truth, you will be breaking an '*ought*'-principle to which I hereby subscribe' (in which I have substituted '*ought*' for the previous 'ought') there is a live imperative element. But in the sentence 'At the very moment when most people (myself included) would agree in saying "He *ought* to have been arriving at the play", he was, &c.', this imperative element, though not dead, is moribund.

It is not dead, because the difference between 'I hereby subscribe' and 'I would agree' is only one of degree; and thus in saying that I would agree that he *ought* to have been arriving, I am in a way saying that he *ought* to have been arriving. Whether my remark is to be taken as primarily informative or primarily evaluative in intention is a matter of very subtle emphasis. Thus, by this further definition, we have succeeded in giving to '*ought*' some of the flexibility between evaluative and descriptive uses which 'ought' has in ordinary language.

One might claim that, if we really were suddenly deprived of the use of the ordinary value-words, we might in time, by using my substitute value-words, come to use them with the same subtlety as we used the old ones; the tool, as I have made it, has a rough feel, but might become more handy with use.

A further objection might be made to '*ought*' as a substitute for 'ought'. It might be said that '*ought*'-sentences would somehow lack the 'authority' which attaches to 'ought'-sentences in ordinary language. When I used '*ought*', I should be only *telling* people to do a certain kind of act; but when in ordinary language I say that they ought to do a certain kind of act, it is not just I that am telling them; I am appealing to a principle that is in some sense there already; it is, as moral philosophers are constantly saying, objective. This is not the place to reiterate at length what I have said many times already, that moral judgements cannot be merely statements of fact, and that if they were, they would not do the jobs that they do do, or have the logical characteristics that they do have. In other words, moral philosophers cannot have it both ways; either they must recognize the irreducibly prescriptive element in moral judgements, or else they must allow that moral judgements, as interpreted by them, do not guide actions in the way that, as ordinarily understood, they obviously do. Here it will suffice to point out that what I have called the descriptive force which moral judgements acquire, through the general acceptance of the principles on which they rest, is quite sufficient to account for the feeling we have that, when we appeal to a moral principle, we are appealing to something that is there already. In a sense it is indeed there already, if our fathers and grandfathers for unnumbered generations have all agreed in subscribing to it, and no one can break it without a feeling of compunction bred in him by years of education. If everyone would agree—with complete conviction—that a certain kind of act ought not to be done, then in saying that it ought not to be done I do indeed speak with an authority which is not my own. And my knowledge that I speak with authority—that I do not need to do more than subscribe to a principle that is already well established—is in a sense a knowledge of fact. But we must, nevertheless, carefully distinguish between two elements in the judgement. That the principle is well-established (i.e. that everyone would agree with it) and that I have feelings of compunction if I break it, are facts; but when I *subscribe* to the principle, I do not state a fact, but make a moral decision. Even if I make it by default—even if I just accept without thinking the standards in which I have been brought up—nevertheless I am, in an important sense, making myself responsible for the judgement. And this means that, if it is an evaluative judgement at all, I cannot just take it as given. As Kant saw, judgements which are properly moral must rest upon 'the property the will has of being a law to itself (independently of every property belonging to the objects of volition)'.[1]

I would ask the reader, in conclusion, to recall what was said at the end of the first part of this book. There, after asking, by what kinds of reasoning, and from what premises, we could arrive at answers to the question 'What shall I do?' I gave an account of how the moral principles are established on which such reasoning must rest; and after saying that 'ought'-sentences might express such principles, I ended 'To become morally adult is . . . to learn to use "ought"-sentences in the realization that they can only be verified by reference to a standard or set of principles which we have by our own decision accepted and made our own'. Thus we have now arrived at a point where we can see clearly, how the discussion of the logic of value-words in Parts II and III of this book is connected with the discussion of the imperative mood in Part I. If the analysis of *'ought'* which I have just sketched

---

[1] *Groundwork*, tr. H. J. Paton, p. 108.

bears any close relation to the use of 'ought' in ordinary language, it shows how it is that moral judgements provide reasons for acting in one way rather than another. And to show this, I conceive to be one of the chief purposes of ethical inquiry.

INDEX

Getting to and telling to, 13–15.

'Good': analytical model of, 183–7; applied to different classes of objects, 96–99, 133, 140, 144; contrasted with 'better than', 183–6; contrasted with descriptive words, 81, 95–110, 111–16, 130–2; contrasted with 'right' and 'ought', 144 f., 151–3, 185; descriptive and evaluative meaning of, 110, 118–26, 146, 148–50; explaining meaning of, 95–110; intrinsic and instrumental uses of, 98, 102 f., 137–40, 160–2; moral and non-moral uses of, 137, 140–5, 161 f.; naturalistic definitions of, 82–93, 145; non-commendatory uses of ('inverted-commas', ironic, conventional), 124–6, 135, 147–9; not the name of common property, 97–99, 103, 106; used to commend, 79, 85, 89–93, 116, 127, 140, 146–50.

Hall, E. W., vii.
Hart, H. L. A., 54.
Heteronomy of the will, 29 f., 70 f., 196.
Hofstadter, A., 26 n.
Hume, 29, 44 f.

Imperative mood, enriched, 187–92.

Imperative sentences: attempts to reduce to indicatives, 5–9; attempts to reduce to expressions of wish or attitude, 9–12; can be used in inferences, 25–28; distinguished from indicatives, 17–20; distinguished from moral judgements, 2 f., 175–9, 187–90; entailed by value-judgements, 29 f., 163–72, 179, 192; function of, not causal, 12–16; governed by logical rules, 24–28; hypothetical, 7, 28, 33–38, 66, 100, 160, 193; may be analytic or self-contradictory, 22–24, 134 f., 174 f.; never completely universal, 3, 177–9, 187 f.; not derivable from indicatives alone, 28–31, 32, 43, 171; refer to states of affairs, 22; universal, 2 f., 11, 25, 28, 134 f., 175–9; see also Principles.

Indicative and imperative sentences, 4–9, 17–22.

Inference: deductive, 32, 38–42; dependent on meaning, 24 f., 33, 47; loose, 45–54; non-verbal, 63 f; rules of, 24 f., 47–49.

Intuition, 30, 64, 74–78, 165, 170.

Inverted commas, 18, 38, 124, 164, 167 f., 170, 173, 194.

Irony, 121, 125, 149.

Justification of actions, 68 f.

Kant, 16, 29, 45, 70, 160, 173, 196.

Learning and teaching, 2, 60–68, 71–78, 134–6, 147–50, 157–60, 193.

Leibniz, 128.

Logical words, 21, 24–27, 32, 47.

Logics, alternative, 23, 27, 192.

Looseness: alleged, of evaluative inferences, 45; of principles, 49–54; of value-words, 115, 184.

McKinsey, J. C. C., 26 n.

Meaning: explaining, 95–110, 114, 132; inference dependent on, 24 f., 33, 47; two senses of, 109, 114, 117–18, 162.

Mention and use, 18, 124 f., 194 f.

Modal sentences, 20 f., 27 n.

Moore, G. E., 30, 82–86, 173.

Moral and non-moral uses of value-words, 140–5, 161 f.

Moral judgements: compared with universal imperatives, 175–9; covertly universal, 129, 154–6, 176; not propaganda, 14–16;